Copyright © 2003 Leon Zeldis
All Rights Reserved

ISBN: 0-935633-27-8

Published by
Anchor Communications
Lancaster, VA 22503, USA
http://www.goanchor.com

MASONIC SYMBOLS AND SIGNPOSTS

Leon Zeldis, 33°

**Past Sovereign Grand Commander
Supreme Council AASR of Israel**

About the Author

León Zeldis was born in Buenos Aires in 1930, son of Russian immigrants. A few months after his birth, the family moved to Chile, where he spent his childhood and youth. He studied Textile Engineering in Philadelphia (USA) and after returning to Chile married Luisa Drapkin. In 1962 the couple, with their four children immigrated to Israel, where they live at present.

Brother Zeldis has published numerous articles and stories in Spanish and English. In 1994 a collection of his poems: Versos Tempranos y Tardíos, was published in Tel Aviv. In 1999, a collection of short stories: El Mar Muerto y Otros Cuentos, appeared in Madrid, Spain, published by Parteluz Editors. In 2002, a new collection of poems: Tan Largo el Olvido, appeared in Mexico.

He is an active Mason, initiated in Chile in 1959. He is Founder and Past Master of La Fraternidad Lodge in Tel Aviv. Filled various posts in the Grand Lodge of Israel and the Scottish Rite, where he reached the highest rank, being elected Sovereign Grand Commander of the Supreme Council of Israel in 1996.

He has published over 150 articles and several books on the history and symbolism of Freemasonry, is an international lecturer on these subjects, and is a founding member of the Chair of Philosophical and Masonic Studies Dr. René García Valenzuela at La República University, in Santiago, Chile. He is a Fellow of the Philalethes Society, member of the Blue Friars, and honorary member of several Masonic research bodies.

He has been Honorary Consul of Chile in Tel Aviv since 1963, and was awarded the Order Bernardo O'Higgins by the Chilean Government.

E-mail address: lzeldis@netvision.net.il

MASONIC SYMBOLS AND SIGNPOSTS

Contents

Introduction: The Value of Symbolism vii

1. The Hiramic Legend and the Symbolism of the ... 1
   Master's Degree

2. Symbolism of the Stone 10

3. Symbolism of the Ladder 24

4. Color Symbolism in Freemasonry 51

5. The Symbolism of Colors in the 69
   Ancient and Accepted Scottish Rite

6. The Labyrinth 82

7. Saints John, Solstices and Freemasonry 91

8. The Opening Ritual 95

9. Campanella's *City of the Sun* 101

10. An Esoteric View of the Rose-Croix Degree 109

11. The Dead Sea Scrolls 122

12. King Solomon's Quarries 137

13. Some Sephardic Jews in Freemasonry 141

14. Projecting the Values of 153
    Freemasonry in Society

15. Education as the Key to Tolerance 162

INTRODUCTION: THE VALUE OF SYMBOLISM

Ours is an age of materialism and high-tech. Science explores every little corner of the universe, from the level of elementary particles to that of galaxies and the boundless universe, overwhelming us with an endless flood of facts, while imagination is banished to the sidelines of fiction. Then, if this is our current situation, why do Freemasons insist in conveying their messages through the medium of symbolism? Why do we continue performing long and complicated ceremonies? Why is Ritual the foundation of masonic teaching? Why, in the scale of Scottish Rite degrees, do we have to perform a special symbolic ceremony to advance from one to another?

The physicist, the modern demiurge, manages his invisible particles in a world of infinitely precise measurements, elaborate instruments, powerful computers and mathematical analysis.

However, the human mind does not appear to work following the rules of computer logic; rather, it works on the basis of symbolic structures. Apprehension and abstraction are symbolic in nature. The language we use to reason with and to convey information is a generally accepted system of symbols. Words do not correspond to measurable physical entities. They are but shadows, images that flash in the mind and evoke associations, memories and expectations. Furthermore, most of the brain's activity goes on underneath the surface, so to say, below the level of consciousness. This activity, revealed sometimes in dreams and myths is nothing but symbols and analogies.

Say I am holding in my hand the score for Beethoven's Fifth Symphony. You see a book, yet in your mind you hear the four starting notes of the music, destiny knocking at the door, or V for Victory, if you remember the Second World War. I say this is a symphony, but a scientist might claim that it is only an object weighing 400 grams, composed of wood pulp beaten into sheets, partly covered with a mixture of carbon black and glue. Who is closer to the truth? Which truth is closer to us?

I now pick up a plastic disk and say this too is Beethoven's Fifth. In my mind, they are closely related, the book and the disk are almost twins. More surprising still, they are both somehow representations of another, totally different experience, the actual concert performance of the music. The human mind has this extraordinary ability to abstract these various experiences: attending a concert, listening to a recording, reading a score, and comprising them into a single symbol: Beethoven's Fifth.

Symbols, then, are tools for thought, ways to grasp reality and to relate it to ourselves. We sometimes forget that all measurements started as proportions of the human body. An inch (a thumb's length), a palm (breadth or length of a hand), a foot, a fathom (length of outstretched arms). The scientist has dehumanized his measurements, because his work is not done with tools adapted to the human body, but with instruments adapted to the machine.

In Masonry we look back to our human dimensions. The symbolic tools we use are intended to reveal direct insights about man, the microcosm, and the world about, the macrocosm. Masonry does not teach like in a classroom. We have no professors, but we all are apprentices, learning through work, through practice, through personal experience.

Masonic teachings are acquired and developed only by personal effort and involvement, by experiencing the ritual ceremonies. Masonic degrees cannot be received by mail or through the Internet, like diplomas after concluding a course of study. Ritual and symbol are dead letter when on the printed page. Only when the words and actions come to life, only by personally experiencing the ceremonies they become reality.

Masons assemble in lodge in order to work. Opening the lodge it is called to labor. We hold work is such high esteem, because work is essentially a personal experience. Working we must use our hands, minds and heart.

Seeing only the external aspects of ritual, one may be inclined to call it a theatrical game. Indeed, when ritual is performed without proper preparation, as a charade, a series of actions, words and gestures carried out without thought, ritual becomes a parody.

But ritual can also become the key to unlock a deeper, more immediate understanding of human nature than can be imparted by logical discourse. Ritual incorporates the accumulated experience of wise men who lived in ages before science and the scientific method were dominant, an experience expressed in legends and symbols. When Freemasonry itself is considered as a philosophical institution, that is, and association of free men lovers of knowledge, then, and only then, can we begin to appreciate the value of ritual and symbol in our work.

Yes, we do play a game in Masonry. It is a very ancient game, ever full of surprises. It is called the game of life. The tools that Masonry puts in our hands allow us to play the game better, with personal enjoyment and for the benefit of mankind.

I have given this book the title '**Masonic Symbols and Signposts**' to stress the fact that Masonic symbolism must be taken as our true 'landmarks'. That is, signs to mark the boundaries of our actions. They point the way, but are not to be taken as impassable barriers. Masonic tradition should act as a compass, not an anchor.

Chapter 1

THE HIRAMIC LEGEND AND THE SYMBOLISM OF THE MASTER'S DEGREE

This chapter is not concerned with the history of the Master's degree, or the three-degree system in general, but rather with the meaning of the Hiramic legend which, as we know, lies at the core of this degree that embodies the Masonic version of the final stage of Initiation. A short bibliography at the end will be of help to those interested in pursuing further their investigation.

We have no certainty about the exact date when the third degree began to be worked but, as far back as 1711, the Trinity College (Dublin) MS mentions three separate classes of Brethren: Entered Apprentices, Fellow Craftsmen and Masters, each with its own secrets.[1]

By 1730, when Prichard's Masonry Dissected was published[2], the three-degree system had become firmly established. The introduction of the Hiramic legend in Masonic ritual dates from the same period, as proven by the advertisement for sale in 1726 of a publication entitled The Whole History of the Widow's Son Killed by the Blow of a Beetle.[3]

The Name Hiram

The name Hiram appears in Masonic manuscripts much earlier, even centuries before, but we have no indication that the medieval mason was familiar with any tragic legend associated to that name, which appears with different spellings such as Anyone, Aman, Amon, Aymon and Hyman.

As with many other names in our rituals, we must look for its source in the Bible. There, we meet some difficulty because of the possible confusion between Hiram, king of Tyre, and the widow's son - Hiram Abif - sent to King Solomon in Jerusalem. Furthermore, the Masonic manuscripts I just mentioned may refer not to Hiram but to the Hebrew word for a craftsman or artificer: Aman or Ooman.

Much has been written about the meaning of the craftsman's name: Hiram Avi or Abif. First, we must understand that the name that appears in the Hebrew Bible has no 'f'. It appears once as 'Avi' (aleph-beth-iod) and elsewhere as 'Aviv' (aleph-beth-iod-vav). The simple or obvious translation would be 'my father' and 'his father', respectively. However, this would have no logical explanation. The Hiram sent to Jerusalem could not be the father of the Tyrian King. The root word 'av', however, has another, less usual meaning. In Genesis 4:8 Joseph tells his brothers that 'God made me father to Pharaoh, lord of his entire household and ruler of all Egypt.' Father ('av' in the original Hebrew), in this sense has the meaning of 'councilor' or 'right-hand man'. It is more plausible that the king of Tyre would send a trusted advisor, capable of organizing and managing the complicated work of building Solomon's Temple.

The Legend

The reader is presumably familiar with the Hiramic legend as exemplified in the third-degree working. We should keep in mind, however, that like most myths, the legend is larger than any one specific recounting. Some features of Hiram Abif's sacrifice have been eliminated from some Masonic rituals, while appearing in other degrees, particularly the 4th to 14th Degrees of the Scottish Rite, belonging to the Lodge of Perfection.

Another word of caution. When studying a mythical tale, we should not expect to find logic or coherence. Each and every detail of the myth has a symbolic explanation, or several; in the course of time, the story is embroidered and additions are made that not always tally with the rest. For example, we are told that the death of Hiram Abif resulted in the loss of the true secrets of the Master Mason, but we are also told that King Solomon and King Hiram of Type shared those secrets. This is an obvious contradiction, yet such is the nature of myth. We must accept it as it has been handed down to us.

Hiram's Murder

The hours high-twelve (noon) and midnight figure prominently in the legendary recounting of Hiram Abif's murder. Not surprisingly, these are the ritual hours of work in the first three degrees of the Ancient and Accepted Scottish Rite.

Noon is the hour when the sun is at the zenith and bodies on earth cast no shadow. There is full illumination (enlightenment). Midnight, on the other hand, is symbolically the end of time and its beginning. The clock returns to zero and a new day begins.

The ruffians are three evil workers driven by ambition, envy and ignorance. Their names vary according to the texts. Here are some of the variations:

Ahiram, Romvel, Gravelot or Hobbden.
Giblon, Giblas, Giblos.
Jubelas, Jubelos, Jubelum.
Methuselah, Amrou, Phanor.[4]
Starke, Sterkin, Austerfuth or Oterfut.

The abundance of alternative names is remarkable. The same phenomenon can be observed in other, non-Masonic initiation legends, as we shall see below.

The Number Five

The raising of Hiram's body (or his surrogate) is connected with the five Points of Fellowship. The number five has a rich lore of symbolism attached to it. To begin with, the number five was held high in the highest esteem by the Pythagoreans, who called it 'Hygeia', that is Health. It was regarded as the conjunction of the first 'female' number - 2 - and the first 'male' number - 3, thus being associated with marriage, or the mystic nuptials. One, the unit, was not considered to be a number at all.

Five is related to the pentagram or pentalpha, that magic five-pointed star associated everywhere with the occult. One of its properties is that every straight line in the pentagram is divided by the others in the golden section. The number five also appears in the legend as the number of fellow-crafts sent to look for Hiram: three groups of five craftsmen each.

Jones mentions that in the 16th and 17th centuries there was much public discussion on the five points, but these referred not to fellowship but to the five points of doctrine to which Calvinism had been reduced.

Five is the hypotenuse of the smallest Pythagorean triangle, that is, a right-angle triangle with integral sides. The Pythagoreans also associated this triangle with marriage, and the Pythagoras Theorem was also known as the Theorem of the Bride.[5] Five is also the fifth Fibonacci number.

The Fibonacci series is an amazing sequence of numbers[6] that appears everywhere in nature, connected with processes of growth and spiral shapes, among others. Many flowers have five petals, and fruits often have five compartments. Five, according to Plutarch, was also called nature by the Pythagoreans, because it is also automorphic, that is, all powers of five end with the digit 5. He also claimed that 'panta' (universe) comes from 'penta' (five).

Five is the first prime of the form $6n - 1$. All primes, except 2 and 3, are one more or one less than a multiple of 6. Five is the second Fermat number and the second Fermat prime. Only 5 Fermat primes are known to exist. Every number is the sum of 5 positive or negative cubes in an infinite number of ways.

There are 5 Platonic solids:[7] the regular tetrahedron, cube, octahedron, dodecahedron and icosahedron. Euclid showed that there are no more than five. The square pyramid is a five-sided solid (pentahedron).

Five, then, is a number connected with life, growth, renewal and eternity.

The question comes to mind, for what particular reason should 5 figure so prominently in the third degree, when the Masonic age of the Master Mason (in the Scottish Rite) is 'seven years . . .' It is the Fellow-craft whose symbolic age is five, and five appears repeatedly in his ritual: five orders of architecture, the five senses, etc. Even the blazing star, with the letter G, which is actually a pentagram, belongs to the second degree and not the third.

The most plausible explanation for these discrepancies is the fact that originally Masonic rituals comprised at most two degrees, and possibly a single ritual divided into several parts. Another vestige of this situation is the fact that, in England at least, the installation ceremony for a new Master of the lodge is conducted in the second degree. In Scotland we find another peculiarity - Scots, after all, must demonstrate their independence! - the Mark Master degree, although given only to Master Masons, is worked within the lodge opened in the Second Degree.

The Substitute Words

Although their Hebrew origin is unquestionable, the Master's words have become corrupted and their exact meaning cannot be decided with certainty. The most plausible explanation, in this author's view, is that both refer to Hiram's death, one coming close to the Hebrew for 'the builder is dead' ('met haboneh') and the other for 'your son is dead' ('met benech'), as if addressing a woman. A Scottish pronunciation would make the close relation of the words clearer. The Hebrew 'met' can become 'mat' as in 'shachmat' (chess: literally 'the Shah is dead').

Jones (see the Bibliography at the end) mentions that in a Christian Dictionary printed in 1678, there are definitions for certain alternative Hebrew words which, we are told, mean 'the smiting of his son', 'the poverty of understanding' or 'the smiting of the builder' (p. 305). We can safely dismiss the middle explanation as misinformation, but the other two coincide rather closely with the explanation advanced above.

An interesting feature that must be noted is that both words now in use can be represented by the initial letters M and B,[8] which leads to the thought that perhaps both words have a common origin. Mendoza proposes a different theory, suggesting a Christian origin to the words, but he appears to be in the minority. As to why two words are in use, and not only one as in the first two degrees, it seems that before the joining of the two rival English Grand Lodges in 1813, the Ancients used one word while the Moderns used the other.[9] As no agreement could be reached to choose one word, a compromise was reached and both were left in use. Mendoza gives more details.

The Wider Context

Let us now examine Hiram's legend within the wider context of world mythology and religion. Some elements of the story are common to many mysteries in which a god or an extraordinary human being suffers death in order to be reborn to a higher state of existence. Let me list some of the more or less common features:
-The element of special wisdom or knowledge possessed by the victim.
-The element of betrayal.
-Burial and putrefaction or dismemberment of the body.
-Searching for the body or grave.
-Raising the body for identification or for a second burial.
-Vengeance and/or punishment of the perpetrator(s).
It has been suggested that Hiram's story may have been derived from the ancient foundation sacrifices, in which a human being was immured in the foundation of an intended structure, to provide it with a 'guardian soul.'
What is clear is that the Hiramic legend belongs in the tradition of classical initiation ceremonies, representing death and rebirth.
Anthropologists have described such rites in all cultures, and historians have transmitted to us similar solemnities in the ancient world, from Egypt, Persia, Greece and Rome. 'To die is to be initiated,' wrote Plutarch, making a play of words between teleutan and telesthai.[10] We could transpose the words, saying that to be initiated is to die... in order to be born again.
Cuneiform texts from Mesopotamia, seven or eight thousand years old, already relate that Dammouzi (Tammuz), the lover of the goddess Ishtar, had been swallowed by the underworld, the kingdom of the dead, the country from which there is no return, the abode of darkness. Ishtar, known as 'widow of the

Son of life' (another widow!) undertakes to release him and bring him back to life, which she does by going through a graded series of trials.

Among the Phoenicians, this myth became that of Astarte and Adonis. Adonis was the lover of Nature, that is, Astarte, who wept his death and finally resurrected him. Every spring, funeral ceremonies were held at Byblos (a city with particular relevance to Installed Masters). Weeping women tore their clothing and wounded their breasts, running about desperately, as if looking for someone. An empty coffin was placed in the temple, ready to receive the body, represented by a wooden statue that was first hidden, and then placed within the coffin. Towards the end of autumn the festival was repeated, with an important difference: grief and lamentations lasted for seven days, but on the eighth mourning gave way to uninhibited joy. The god had been reborn and ascended to heaven.

The Adonis of Phrygia was called Attis or Papas, the divine shepherd, consort of Cybele or Maa, goddess of the earth. The mysteries of Cybele were brought to Rome after the end of the Punic wars, and were celebrated in the eternal city with increasing enthusiasm during six hundred years.

In Egypt we find the myth of Isis and Osiris, too well known to repeat here.

The Greeks had not one, but several version of these legends. One, the mysteries of Cabires, in Samothrace, included the dramatic representation of the history of three brothers: Axieros, Axiokersos and Axiokersa (note the alliteration!). According to the version reported by Firmicus Maternus, two of the Cabires killed the third and buried him at the foot of Mount Olympus. He was then brought back to life by Hermes, the god of the occult. Some Etruscan mirrors have engraved on the back scenes of this drama. In one, we see Axieros seized by his two brothers, before two columns with Corinthian capitals. In another, Hermes, accompanied by two satyrs serving as his assistants, approaches the corpse and tries to raise it with the help of his magic wand. The Cabires, like Hiram, are of Phoenician origin.

In the mysteries of Mithra, as well, the initiate was symbolically killed. Once, the emperor Commodus who was officiating as mystagogue - the conductor of the dead - got carried away by the drama and actually murdered the luckless initiate. Fortunately, no such mishap has ever happened in a Masonic ceremony!

The Dionysian mysteries, also very popular in Rome, as in the Eastern provinces of the empire, featured the dismemberment of Dionysus, later reassembled and resurrected by Zeus.

Some of these rites continued for many centuries after the spread of Christianity, sometimes disguised under a Christian cloak. D'Alviella (p. 77) mentions, for example, a ceremony held in the island of Malta in the 16th century, as recounted by an Arab writer. At the time of the feast of St. John, which coincided with the flowering of beans, the priests hid a statue of the saint under branches of flowering beans. The saint was then mourned as if dead. After three days, his return was celebrated; the statue was uncovered and carried in procession to the church. It is not difficult to perceive that the saint was acting as a surrogate for Dionysus.

The role of initiation in human society can be best summarized by quoting Mircea Eliade (p. 220): 'Initiation appears in all authentic human existence, for two reasons: on the one hand, because all authentic human life implies deep crises, trials, anguish, loss and recovery of the self, "death and rebirth"; on the other, because, no matter how full, all existence appears, at a certain moment, as an unfilled promise.'

'This is not a moral judgment about the past, but a vague feeling of having missed the vocation, of having betrayed the best within oneself. In such moments of total crisis, one hope only seems capable of providing salvation: the hope of being able to start life again. That is, in short, that we dream of a new existence, renewed, plentiful, and meaningful... The nostalgia of an initiatic renovation which arises sporadically in the heart of hearts of modern irreligious man, seems to us, therefore, as most significant: it would be, in the final analysis, the modern expression of man's eternal longing to find a positive meaning to death, to accept death as a rite of passage to a superior state of being.'

'If initiation can be said to be a distinctive dimension of human existence, this is due, above all, to the fact that only initiation assigns a positive task to death; to prepare the new birth, purely spiritual, access to a mode of being secure from the ravages of time.'

Selected Bibliography:

Beresniak, Daniel, *La Legende d'Hiram et les Initiations Traditionelles*, E. Detrad, Paris 1987.

Eliade, Mircea, *Birth and Rebirth*, Harper & Row, New York 1958.

Goblet D'Alviella, *Des Origines du Grade de Maitre dans la Franc-Ma(onnerie*, Guy Tredaniel, Paris 1983.

Jones, Bernard E., *Freemason's Guide and Compendium*, Harrap, London 1950.

Mendoza, Harry, "*The Words of a Master Mason*", Ars Quatuor Coronatorum, Vol. 102, 1989, p. 164.

Wells, David, *The Penguin Dictionary of Curious and Interesting Numbers*, London 1986 (reprinted 1988).

Chapter Notes

1. Jones, p. 242.
2. Actually a small booklet of only 26 pages.
3. Jones, p. 318.
4. Nerval, Gerard de, *Journey to the Orient*, Chapter 12: Makbenah.
5. Well, p. 58.
6. A series in which each term is the sum of the two previous terms. It was christened the Fibonacci sequence by Eduard Lucas in 1877.
7. A polyhedron formed by equal plane faces that can be enclosed in a sphere.
8. Master Masons' aprons used in Scottish Rite lodges have the letters *M* and *B* on the front.
9. This explanation appears in the 1762 exposure *Jachin and Boaz*, quoted by Mendoza.
10. Goblet D'Alviella, p. 65.

Chapter 2

THE SYMBOLISM OF STONE

Preamble

A fundamental question, rarely asked, is the reason why our forerunners, the Brethren who wrote and developed the complicated symbolic structures of moral and philosophical teachings we now know as speculative Freemasonry, would choose to base their system on such modest materials as the builder's trade, his tools and legends. Such activities as seafaring, metalworking, agriculture and husbandry, among others, could have been used just as well in developing a "peculiar system of morality veiled in allegory and illustrated by symbols." Indeed, they have been used for this purpose at one time or another, by various individual thinkers and organizations.

I hope to show that the stonemason's trade, and his material - stone - have such profound, far-reaching and universal significance and connotations that the choice was not only justified but inevitable.

It is my belief that a study of the rich symbolism of stone will illuminate many facets of Freemasonry and will lead to a better understanding of our rituals and traditions.

Introduction

Stone has been, from prehistoric times, the principal material used to build and adorn important structures, where solidity and permanence are the paramount considerations. Stone became paradigmatic of stability, hardness and endurance in all languages, bearing a wealth of symbolic meaning, with many deep-rooted psychological and historical associations and suggestions, some of which will be examined later.

The scientific or chemical definition of stone is of no concern to us. Suffice it to say that stone is the nonmetallic component of rock and that it appears in many forms, colors and degrees of hardness and brittleness. Stones are used for construction and jewelry, for sculpture and for industry.

Stone, having a chemical structure, reacts with the atmosphere. It may change color, erode, combine with different airborne chemicals. It 'ages' both chemically and physically, due to the release of the stresses to which it had been subjected in the geologic past. 'Granite blocks can increase in compressive strength by a third in only six months aging through recovery from the natural pre-stressing'. [1]

All these phenomena must have appeared to men of an earlier age as proof that stone was not totally inert, but held a certain form of life.

Stone in Antiquity

Stone was in all probability the first material used by primitive man. The first coarse tools were simply rough stones used to hammer, cut and grind. The first giant step taken by mankind toward civilization was the change from using natural stones to chip or flaked implements and weapons, with improved cutting edges, or allowing the use of a handle. By this apparently simple act, of modifying a stone before using it as a tool, homo sapiens became homo faber and started to fashion his environment, instead of being the passive user of what nature had to offer.

Stones were not only used as tools, but became the object of veneration of primitive men, whose survival depended on them. 'Rubbing and polishing stones is a well-known, exceedingly ancient activity of man. In Europe, holy stones, wrapped in bark and hidden in caves, have been found in many places; as containers of divine powers they were probably kept there by men of the Stone Age. At the present time, some of the Australian aborigines believe that their dead ancestors continue to exist in stones as virtuous and divine powers, and that if they rub these stones, the power increases (like charging them with electricity) for the benefit of both the living and the dead.' [2]

The belief in 'living stones' or stones having a soul, is not restricted to barbarous tribes. An astonishing number of primitive myths describe man as born of stone. [3] In the myth of

Deucalion and Pyrrha, the Greek parallel to the biblical story of the flood, the earth is repopulated by Deucalion throwing 'his mother's bones' (stones) over his shoulder.

Many holy stones existed in antiquity. In Greece they were called baetylus or baetulus, a name probably derived from the Hebrew bethel (beit-el, house of God). The stone was regarded as the abiding place or symbol of a god. "The most famous example is the holy stone at Delphi, the omphalos ("navel") that reposed in the temple of Apollo and supposedly marked the exact center of the universe." [4]

Many gods were born of rocks, such as Mithras, whose cult was the main competitor of Christianity in the early centuries of our era. Stone was conceived as petra genitrix, assimilated to the Great Goddess, the matrix mundi. The parallels between caverns, the inside of the earth, and the womb, are too obvious to stress. The interior of the earth was conceived by the ancients as a place of gestation, where life germinates and develops. The same germinal sense of the earth appears in many rites and myths of growth, like that of Demeter that figured in the Eleusian Mysteries. Caverns, with their womb connotation, were regarded as sacred places and oracles usually dwelt in them.

Rock was considered not only a living organism, as mentioned before, but as developing inside the earth. Precious stones, in Hindu mythology, are differentiated by their age. Diamond is the most 'mature' stone, while emeralds and rubies are still insufficiently developed. [5]

Metals, too, were regarded as maturing within the womb of the earth. Gold was the mature or perfect metal, into which all others slowly evolved or ripened. The alchemist, according to this view, had only to find a way of accelerating this maturation process in his laboratory to achieve within a short time what in nature takes eons. For this, he required a special ingredient, what in modern chemistry is called a catalyst, which would serve to accelerate the evolution from base metal into gold. This ingredient was called by alchemists 'the philosopher's stone'.

Stone, then, is the key to the growth or metamorphosis of the other elements. In Continental Lodges, the Chamber of Reflections is where the candidate waits and meditates in solitude before his initiation, is adorned, among other things, with a picture of a cock (representing Mercury - Hermes, about whom more below), and the legend V.I.T.R.I.O.L., which are the capital letters of a Latin inscription meaning 'Visit the depths of the earth and rectifying (i.e., purifying) thou shall find the hidden stone'.

Initiation is, in a sense, a ceremony of purification or refining, and the divestiture of metals is connected with this concept. This aspect of the Masonic initiation is also explained by the belief that metal is somehow related to the demonic and magical side of nature, while stone is connected with its positive aspects. This idea is explored by Mircea Eliade in his book already quoted. A further embodiment of this conception is the injunction against placing metallic objects over the Volume of the Sacred Law. Some Lodges go so far as to have square and compasses especially made of wood for this purpose.

The Germanic tribes, too, believed that the spirit of the dead continued living in their tombstones. The Jewish custom of placing stones on graves may spring partially from the symbolic idea that something eternal, part of the dead person, remains and can be represented most fittingly by a stone. Stone symbolizes the simplest and deepest experience - the experience of something eternal.[6] For stone as a symbol of the self, Jung's works can be consulted.[7]

The body of a dead person is returned to the bosom of the earth in order to continue its evolution. Maximum contact with the earth is ensured by not using a coffin, as in Orthodox Jewish burial rites. It will be noted that H.A., likewise, was interred directly within the earth, without a casket.

Stone gods, or stone monuments erected as god-images or places of worship, have been known from the earliest antiquity. It will be sufficient to mention the many menhirs and dolmens dotting the landscape of Europe. Perhaps the most famous site of this kind is Stonehenge, on Salisbury plain (England), which comprises several concentric circles of stones, apparently built for astronomical and ritual purposes between 2350 and 1350 B.C.

E. Sidney Hartland believes that 'many of the menhirs in Europe and Asia Minor have probably been actually figures of deities. Rocks, boulders and standing stones have been worshiped as gods or as inhabited by gods all over the world. Wherever men have been struck by the appearance or position of a rock formation or a stone, they have regarded it with awe as uncanny, and in innumerable cases they have ultimately erected it into a divinity, brought offerings and put up prayers before it. Instances need not be cited; they are found in every quarter of the globe.'[8]

In his book Ritual, from which the previous quotation was taken, Theodor Reik adds numerous examples of stone regarded as a god. Furthermore, Reik puts forward the theory that the Tables of the Law, received by Moses on Mount Sinai, were actually stone gods, which were ritually murdered by Moses. This was later recorded as the breaking of the stone tablets in an act of fury caused by the people's infidelity to Jahve.[9]

The Spanish philologist Ramon Menendez Pidal has commented that 'a very ancient custom exists in many peoples, of travelers signaling the place where a violent death has taken place by throwing a stone and uttering a prayer or a curse, according to the quality of the victim.'[10]

Stones not only lie in the earth, and they also fall from the heavens. In some primitive cultures, the heavens are thought to be made of stone. Aeroliths have been worshiped in many places as divine incarnations (or should we say impetrations?). The stone of Pessinus, a meteorite adored as the Phrygian Great Mother, was brought to Rome at the time of the second Punic War (218-201 B.C.) as result of a sibylline prophecy. It was set up in a temple especially built on the Palatine hill. [11]

The association of stones with divinities explains perhaps their connection with the crowning of kings (who ruled by divine right). Two notable examples are the Irish Lia-Fail, [12] and the Stone of Scone (or Stone of Destiny) on which Scottish Kings were enthroned since the year 838 when Kenneth MacAlpine brought it from Dunstaffnage.

The Romans, when taking an oath, held a stone in their hand to represent the presence of Jupiter (Zeus). It was called the Jupiter lapis.

The same god was also the god of rain and the Romans held a festival called Aquaelicium, during which the priests brought into Rome a cylindrical stone called lapis manalis. It will be remembered that Zeus was saved from being devoured by his father, the titan Cronus (Saturn), by being exchanged for a stone (Abadir). The stone swallowed by Cronus is supposed to have been at the Delphi sanctuary. The mythical equivalent of stone and flesh is remarkably explicit. [13] Such is also the case in the myth of Medusa, the Gorgon, who turned men into stones.

Worshiping the holy stones was common in antiquity. The author Arnobius, mentioning the blind idolatry of his pagan days, says: 'If I ever saw an oiled stone, smeared with oil, I used to worship it, as if some power resided in it.' [14]

The Latin word lapis means not only stone, but also tombstone. Hence the adjective lapidary, meaning suitable to be engraved on a tombstone. Dilapidated, on the other hand, means literally 'with missing stones'.

Hermes and Stone

The Greek god Hermes holds special significance for Freemasons, being a deity closely connected with the underworld and the occult (Hermetic Sciences).

The name of the god itself suggests the word for 'stone' or 'rock' and also the verb which means 'to protect'. [15]

In earliest times, Hermes was venerated in Greece as a 'milestone' in which the spirit of the numen was thought to be hidden. 16 The stone pillars erected in honor of the god were sometimes substituted by stone heaps, particularly at crossroads (something similar was practiced by the Hebrews - see below). Each passerby added a stone to the mound as sign of homage and to invoke the protection of the god, who was not only the guide of all travelers, both in this world and the next, but also the patron of merchants and thieves, which might indicate something about the honesty of ancient Greek merchants!

Hermes was a multifaceted god: the sacrificial herald of the gods, the messenger of Zeus, inventor of music (he invented both the lyre and the shepherd's flute), the patron of gymnastic skills and the god of clever and wise discourse, which are not necessarily coexistent. 'As he is the guide of the living on their way, so is he also the conductor of the souls of the dead in the nether world, and he is as much loved by the gods of those regions as he is by those above. For this reason, sacrifices were offered to him in the event of deaths. Hermea (square pillars terminated generally with a head of Hermes and bearing a phallus) were placed on the graves . . . in general, he was accounted the intermediary between the upper and lower worlds, as he was born in the fourth month, the number four was sacred to him.' 17

Being familiar with the nether world, Hermes was also the god of mining and digging for buried treasure. He was the god of sleep and dreams as well. Little wonder, then, that he is connected with all forms of arcane knowledge, hence called hermetic. Under one of his forms, Hermes Trismegistus (the Thrice-Powerful), he was identified with the Egyptian god Thoth.

Hermes appears in one of the Degrees of the A.A.S.R. and in some Lodges, the staffs of the Deacons are topped with the caduceus, the wand with entwined snakes carried by Hermes.

Stone in Jewish Tradition

I have already mentioned the possible divine nature of the Tablets of the Law. Sacred stones or pillars, called in Hebrew

Matzevot, are already mentioned by Herodotus (5th Century B.C.) and appear in several places in the Old Testament. Jacob, after striking a pact with Laban, erected a stone monument which he called Gal-Ed (Testimonial Pillar). Moses erected twelve stone pillars near the altar of sacrifices. After crossing the Jordan river, Joshua ordered taking twelve stones from the river bed, one for each tribe, setting them up in their camps and carrying them later on their shoulders as memorial of the crossing on dry ground (Joshua 4). Joshua also set up other twelve stones in the middle of the river, in the place where the priests carrying the Ark of the Testimony had stood. Finally, Joshua erected at Gilgal the twelve stones he had brought from the Jordan, so that future generations would know that the Lord had done to the Jordan just what he had done to the Red Sea.

Later, Joshua built an altar on Mount Ebal, made of uncut stones, on which no iron tool had been used (Joshua 8:30-31). At the end, before dying, he wrote down the Law on a large stone he set up under an oak tree in Shechem, as a witness against the people of Israel should they betray their covenant (Joshua 24:26-27).

Samuel put up a stone which he called Eben-Ezer ("Stone of Help") after the Philistines were routed at Mizpah (1 Samuel 7:12). Adoniah offered a sacrifice near the rock of Zohelet ("Joyful"), near the fountain of Rogel (1 Kings 1:9).

We could continue multiplying the examples, but the point is clear: the ancient Hebrews used uncut stones for their ritual monuments and altars. This fact is made clear in Exodus 20:25: 'And if you make me an altar of stone, you shall not build it of hewn stones; for if you wield your tool [literally "sword"] upon it you profane it.'

Jacob's ladder, which figures on the Entered Apprentice's Tracing Board, [18] is directly related to the stone pillar erected by Jacob after his dream. He had used the stone as a pillow and poured a libation of oil to consecrate the memorial (Genesis 28:18). Jacob names Beth-El the place where he had his dream, that is, the house of God. In accordance with Reik's commentary on this episode, the stone itself is an image of God and only thus can its anointment be understood. [19]

This identity of stone, human being and anthropomorphic deity throws light on the saying: "Look to the rock from which you were cut and to the quarry whence you were hewn; look to Abraham your father and to Sarah who gave you birth" (Isaiah 51:1-2). There is a Jewish custom, already mentioned, of placing a small stone over the grave one has visited. This may be connected to the Greek traveler's adding a stone to the Hermes monuments, in order to secure a safe journey. Hermes, as stated, was also the guide of the dead.

Hewing the stone might be construed as injuring the deity. This would explain the ancient injunction against using hewn stones for building an altar. Another instance of this taboo is the fact that while building King Solomon's Temple, no sound of hammers or chisels or any other iron tool was heard at the building site (1 Kings 6:7). All the stone blocks were dressed at the quarry. An interesting possibility was raised in this connection by Bro. William C. Blaine, who noted that the depth of Zedekiah's cavern - known also as King Solomon's Quarry, used to quarry large blocks of stone in ancient times, and which lies under the western section of Jerusalem's Old City, would prevent any noise reaching the site of the Temple on Mount Moriah. [20]

Another important legend connected with this subject is the one relating that Solomon owned a wondrous tool (the shamir worm or stone), created on the Sabbath eve, that could cut any stone. [21]

There is, of course, the famous passage in Psalm 118: "The stone the builders rejected has become the cornerstone (or capstone)." This has become the basis for an entire Degree in Freemasonry.

Stone in Christian Tradition

The best example of the importance of stone in Christian teachings is, of course, the case of Simon the fisherman, whom Jesus calls Peter (Petrus - the stone): "I tell you that you are Peter, and on this rock I will build my church" (Matthew 16:18).

The Pope, as linear successor to Peter, is called Holy Father. The connection between pater (father) and petrus (stone) is obvious. In the Hebrew language as well, the same letters forming the word "father" (av: alef-beth) appear in the word for "stone" (even: alef-beth-noon). Another interesting explanation for the name Peter appears in an old Jewish legend, according to which it was the Christians who gave him that name because he exempted them (en Hebrew: p-t-r) from observing the precepts of the Torah. 22

In another instance, Christ himself is compared to a rock (1 Corinthians 10:4): 'For they drank from the spiritual rocks that accompanied them, and that rock was Christ.' A passage in the book of Revelation (2:17) mentions a white pebble with a secret name written on it, which only the recipient will understand.

According to a story related by Marco Polo in his book of travels, the three Magi received from the infant Jesus a gift in exchange for the gold, myrrh and incense they brought him. This was a small casket which, upon being opened, was revealed to contain a stone. Without realizing the import of the gift, the three oriental kings threw what they believed to be only a worthless stone into a well, whereupon a fire came down from heaven into the well.

Observing the miracle, the kings realized too late that the stone they had discarded was meant to symbolize the strength and constancy in faith that was expected of them. They took with themselves some of the fire from heaven and carried it to their respective countries and this, the legend says, is the origin of the fire-worshipers of Persia. 23

The Holy Grail is described in the Parzival not as a cup, but as a stone of the hardest kind, called lapis exillas, which brings to mind the alchemist's stone. According to another version, the cup was made of emerald (also a kind of stone). 24

Stone in Islamic Tradition

The focal point of worship for a Muslim is the Ka'aba at Mecca. Every pious Muslim must make a pilgrimage to Mecca (the Hadj) at least once in his lifetime, making seven circumambulations around the sanctuary of the Ka'aba, the Black Stone which, according to witnesses' reports, appears to be a meteorite. The pilgrims also throw stones at pillars representing the devil, in the vicinity of Mina.[25]

In Jerusalem, there is a stone in the Dome of the Rock, built on the spot where the Sanctum Sanctorum of the Temple is supposed to have been located, and the spot from which Muhammad is said to have jumped to heaven, mounted on his white mule Al Burak.

Stone in Masonic Literature

In Masonic rituals and legends, stone plays a leading role, beginning with the Entered Apprentice, who is enjoined to polish the rough stone with hammer and chisel, and culminating with the variously-shaped stones appearing in diverse Master Mason and Royal Arch Degrees, there is hardly a ceremony in symbolic Freemasonry which is not connected in some way with stones.

After completion of the initiation ceremony, the new Mason is placed in a particular position within the Lodge and is usually told that he represents the cornerstone on which Freemasonry's spiritual Temple must be built.

Bro. G. W. Speth has provided a wealth of evidence to support the theory that cornerstones had originally a sacrificial character, destined to provide a soul that would protect the new building.[26]

In the course of his advancement, the Entered Apprentice eventually becomes a Master Mason, and then he plays the part of the victim in a crime that, apparently, has little connection with cornerstones.

However, as been noted in the previous chapter on the Hiramic Legend, a possible explanation for this is that it, too, refers to a ritual sacrifice, designed to provide a human soul for King Solomon's Temple. In the initiation ceremony, a person plays the role of cornerstone, while in the builder's ceremony, the stone plays the role of a human victim. The exchangeability of stone and flesh as noted in an earlier section of this paper finds here another application.

In the Edinburgh Register House MS (1696), one of the earliest Masonic documents that have survived, the Jewels of the Lodge include the Perpend Esler and the Broad Ovall. The first, the perpendicular ashlar, is a stone placed crosswise through a wall, while the second is believed to be a corruption of a 'broached dornal', that is, a chiseled stone. [27]

Similar information appears in the Chetwode Crawley MS (c. 1700): 'perpendester' and 'broked-mall'. [28]

The Mason's work is thus described in the Dumfries No 4 MS (c. 1710): 'to work in all manner of worthy work in stone: Temple, Churches, Cloysters, Cities, Castles, Pirimides, Towers & all other worthy buildings of stone'. In the same manuscript we find a reference to the 'two pillars of stone', one that would not sink and the other that would not burn, which held the noble art or science. [29]

The Mason himself, as we have noted, is likened to a stone. In Long Livers, a book published in London in 1722, we find this pithy definition: 'Ye are living stones, built up a spiritual House, who believe and rely on the chief Lapis Angularis, which the refractory and disobedient Builders disallowed . . . '. [30]

The reference, of course, is to the already quoted passage in Psalm 118, used in the Mark Degree. In the Royal Ark Mariner Degree, a porphyry stone is used in place of the Volume of the Sacred Law This refers to one of the myths connected with Noah, which is his discovery of a cave on Mount Moriah in which he found a mysterious stone (presumably a porphyry stone) with certain mystic characters engraved thereon. [31]

I could multiply the examples of stone symbolism in our rituals, but enough has been said already to justify our thesis.

In conclusion, the deep and various meanings of stone as a physical object and as allegory makes it easy to understand why the art of the builder should have been selected as the appropriate vehicle to convey the philosophical and mystical teachings of speculative Freemasonry in its different manifestations.

The Mason, the stone carver, is seen to share many an attribute with the priest and the demiurge, which in Platonic philosophy represents the Architect who fashions the sensible world.

Chapter Notes

1 Winkler, E.M., Stone: properties, durability in man's environment, Springer-Verlag, reviewed by Morrison, Philip, Scientific American, April, 1974, p. 123.
2 Franz, M.L. von, "The Process of Individuation", in Man and his Symbols, ed. by Jung, Carl G., Doubleday & Co. New York 1964, p. 205 and photo on p. 204.
3 See the bibliography in Eliade, Mircea, Forgerons et Alchimistes, Flammarion, Paris, 1956. Note G.
4 Encyclopedia Britannica, sub voc. Baetylus.
5 Eliade, op. cit., Chapter 4, passim.
6 Franz, op. cit., p. 209.
7 See Jung, Carl G., Von den Wurzeln des Bewusstein, Z?rich 1954, pp. 200 seq., 415 seq., 449 seq.
8 Hastings, James, Encyclopaedia of Religion and Ethics, Vol. II, Edinburgh 1920, p. 864. Quoted in Reik, Theodor, Ritual, The International Psycho-Analytical Library, London, 1931.
9 Op. cit., pp. 346-356.
10 Don Ramon Menendez Pidal, "Cordoba y la leyenda de los infants de Lara" in
Los Godos y la Epopeya Espanola, Espasa-Calpe, Madrid 1965, p. 328.
11 Seyffert, Oskar, Dictionary of Classical Antiquities, Meridian Library, New York 1956, sub voc. Rhea.
12 Cirlot, J.E., A Dictionary of Symbols, Dorset Press, New York 1991, p. 314.
13 Seiffert, op. cit., sub voc. Jupiter.
14 Arnobius, Adversus Nationes, i. 39.
15 New Larousse Encyclopedia of Mythology, Hamlyn, London 1959, p. 123.
16 Parodi, Bent, "La pietra come simbolo dello spirito umano", Hiram, No. 12, December 1987, p. 372.
17 Seiffert, op. cit., sub voc. Jupiter.
18 See the next chapter.
19 Reik, op. cit., p. 346.
20 "King Solomon's Quarries", The Israel Scottish Rite, Vol. 3, N° 1, December 1973, p. 23.

21 See Klein, Ernest, A Comprehensive Etymological Dictionary of the Hebrew Language for readers of English, Carta, Jerusalem 1987, p. 666 sub voc. "shamir".

22 Kohn, Moshe, "Succot and St, Peter", The Jerusalem Post, 18 October 1989, p.5.

23 Marco Polo, The travels of Marco Polo, Penguin, London, 1958, pp. 28-29.

24 Pisani, Paolo, "Considerazioni muratori sul Graal", Hiram N° 12, December 1987, p. 371.

25 Gibb, H.A.R., Mohammedanism. Mentor Book, The New American Library, New York 1955, p. 57.

26 Speth, G.W., "Builder's Rites and Ceremonies; the folk-lore of Masonry", A.Q.C., Vol. 89, 1977, pp. 139-168.

27 Knoop, Jones and Hamer, The Early Masonic Catechisms, London 1975, p. 32.

28 Ibid. p. 38.

29 Ibid, pp. 54 and 67.

30 Knoop, Jones and Hamer, Early Masonic Pamphlets, London 1978, p. 44.

31 Batham, C.N., reply to a query, printed in one of the summons of Quatuor Coronati Lodge.,

Chapter 3

SYMBOLISM OF THE LADDER

The ladder is a symbol that appears frequently in religious and esoteric contexts since ancient times. It features prominently in the Tracing Board of the First Degree (Jacob's ladder), and it is also an important symbol both in the Second Degree (the spiral staircase) and in the Thirtieth Degree of the Ancient and Accepted Scottish Rite, Knight Kadosh, (the two-sided ladder).

The importance of the ladder as a symbol of gradual spiritual perfection, exemplified by the first nine degrees of York Rite Masonry, can be judged by the title of a book by Brother John Sherer: The Masonic Ladder, or the Nine Steps to Ancient Freemasonry, being a Practical Exhibit, in Prose and Verse, of the Moral Principles, Precepts, Traditions, Scriptural Instructions and Allegories of the Degrees of Entered Apprentice, Fellow Craft, Master Mason, Mark Master, Past Master, Most Excellent Master, Royal Arch Mason, Royal Master and Select Master. [1]

Spiritual Significance of the Ladder

From remote antiquity, the ladder was taken as a paradigm of spiritual ascent. In a bas-relief from the 3rd Dynasty of Ur, dated c. 2070-1960 B.C., there appears a seven-rung ladder, 'suggesting initiation leading from lower to higher realms of consciousness: above the initiate is the conjunction of a crescent moon and sun, symbolizing the union of masculine and feminine principles as the central meaning of initiation'. [2]

We find here the core of an explanation for the use of the ladder as a symbol in the First Degree of Freemasonry, in preference to others.

We should note, as well, this early example of the conjunction of the ladder with two other important symbols in the lodge: the sun and the moon.

The reason why verticality and ascent are connected with perfection may be the fact that the vertical posture is one of the determinant factors in making man human. As remarked by Guerillot, 'verticality, the high, the heaven, ascent, and all that is connected with them constitute as an imaginary asymptote of rising homo erectus and his descendants.' [3] The spiritual ladder appears in other contexts as well, besides the story of Jacob's dream (about which, see below). '(The ladder) is found in the Pagan Mysteries of Mithras, and in the Mysteries of Brahma, Dr. Oliver found it in the Scandinavian Mysteries. Among the Cabalists, the ladder was represented by the ten Sephirot, though it usually included only seven steps'. [4]

J. Bowing (1819)

In Egypt, according to the Book of the Dead, a ladder enabled seeing the gods. The Egyptian god Horus, son of Isis, was known as the god of the ladder, and small ladders were worn as amulets. [5] This Horus or Harpocrates was represented by the Egyptians as a naked boy with a finger on his mouth. The Greeks misunderstood this symbol of childhood and made him the god of Silence and Secrecy. Later, when the Mysteries were in vogue, his worship was widely extended. [6]

In the Mysteries of Mithras, the ceremonial ladder or 'Climax' had seven rungs, each made of a different metal, corresponding to the seven planets or 'heavens': the first was lead (Saturn), then came tin (Venus), bronze (Jupiter), iron (Mercury), 'monetary alloy' (Mars), silver (Moon) and gold (Sun). While ascending the ladder the initiate traversed in effect the seven heavens to reach the empyrean, in the same way that the last heaven was reached by climbing the seven floors of the Babylonian ziggurat. The initiatory ladder was placed in the Center of the Universe and was the Axis of the World. [7] The reason for placing the foot of Jacob's Ladder on the altar, as depicted in the tracing board, above that central point within a circle, now becomes clear.

'Submission is the characteristics of initiation, but it is not apathy or weakness; it contains a strong element of the archetypal "trial of strength" carried over from the heroic phase of life. This is exemplified in the symbol of the seven stages represented as seven rungs of a ladder leading to Heaven, so that the journey may be an ascent as well as a descent'. [8]

The source of the connection made in Freemasonry between the ladder and the moral virtues can be traced back to the Greek philosophers: 'Man's arduous ascent to God is represented by a ladder. John Klimakos (died c. 600 and whose name means John of the Ladder) laid the foundation for this graduated conception, rooted in neo-Platonism. The starting point of this "ascent to Paradise" is Jacob's dream'.

'Man's task is ... to overcome his sinful desires, then to achieve the virtues, if he wishes to attain in the end the topmost rung and there join the Pauline trinity of virtues, Faith, Hope and Charity'. [9]

The relationship between the ladder symbol and initiation, already noted, can also be traced back to classical antiquity. In The Golden Ass of Apuleius, which is an account of a symbolic initiation, there appears a Stairway of the Seven Planets.

'The initiation of late classic syncretism, already saturated with alchemy (cf. the Vision of Zosimos) was particularly concerned with the theme of ascent through the seven spheres or planets that symbolizes the return of the soul to the sun-god from whom it originated.' [10]

In the course of an examination of the musical expression of the ladder as a symbol of spiritual ascent, R.H. Wells traces the close links between the ladder symbol and another symbol not unconnected with Masonry: the Great Chain of Being. [11]

'The theme of a spiritual ladder is closely connected with the idea of human perfectibility, best expressed in Pico della Mirandola's Oratio de Ominis Dignitate (1486), where Pico imagines the voice of God saying: "We have made thee neither of heaven nor of earth, neither mortal nor immortal, so that with freedom of choice and with honor, as though the maker and molder of thyself, thou mayest fashion thyself in whatever shape thou shalt prefer. Thou shalt have the power to degenerate into the lowest forms of life, which are brutish. Thou shalt have the power, out of thy soul's judgment, to be reborn into the higher forms, which are divine".[12]

In other words, the ascending and descending angels on Jacob's ladder are representations of the soul's capacity to rise or fall along the Chain of Being. As Jean Farre explains: 'The ladder is a bridge between earth and heaven; it enables man to rise in the realm of knowledge and access the sacred...Further, the ladder expresses man's search in his aspiration for progress. In this case, the movement is ascending. However, the movement can also be descending. Man starts then looking for his deep roots, his unconscious, and even hidden knowledge. We could speak here of a descent to the underworld, in order to unveil all secrets, the mysteries that are in man. The ladder then reaches down to the bowels of the earth.' [13]

As explained by Wells, 'The images of ladder, scale and chain are found universally in medieval and Renaissance art, because the cosmos was conceived as a series of interlocking hierarchies. The concept of 'the Great Chain of Being' expresses the order and harmony of the cosmos. This image was conflated with two others: the Golden Chain of Zeus (Iliad, VIII, 19-27) and Jacob's Ladder.'[14]

'The visionary ladder upon which the sleeping Jacob sees angels ascending and descending was widely interpreted as a symbol of cosmic harmony..., Peter Sterry wrote in 1675: "All ranks and degrees of Being so become, like the mystical steps in the scale of Divine Harmony and Proportions, Jacob's Ladder".'

'But the scala naturae, whether seen as a chain or a ladder, was not simply a static symbol of the world order; for pagan and Christian alike, it was a dynamic image expressive of the soul's potential for either amelioration or degeneration. According to St. John Chrysostom (born c. A.D. 347), Jacob's Ladder signified "the gradual ascent by means of virtue, by which it is possible for us to ascend from earth to heaven". Chrysostom's interpretation of Genesis 28:12 is reflected in medieval iconography. Visual representations of the soul's struggle to achieve spiritual perfection commonly portray the individual climbing a ladder accompanied by allegorical figures representing the virtues and vices by which he is assisted or hindered (illustrations 1 and 6).'

Origen, the great theologian of the 3rd century, in his Commentary to the Song of the Songs, describes a seven-step ladder that the soul must ascend in order to celebrate its marriage with the divine Logos.' [15]

Saint John Clymaco (579?-649?) in his Ladder of Paradise, describes a ladder of thirty steps, leading from the depths of profane life, full of temptations, to the heights of divine light. By strange coincidence, the central symbol of the 30th degree of the Scottish Rite is the two-sided ladder (see below).

One of the classic works on the spiritual life, written by the English mystic Walter Hilton (d. in 1396), bears the title The Scale of Perfection, where 'scale' (from Latin 'scala') is used with the meaning of 'ladder'. [16]

'Just as the Golden Chain of Zeus was identified in the Middle Ages with Jacob's Ladder, and both with the scala mundi, so the Platonic ladder of love was conflated with the biblical image of a stairway of the angels. One of the most memorable passages in Dante's Paradiso is the scene in which the poet sees the figure of Beatrice standing on a ladder, which rises into the empyrean, and she steps down beckoning his soul to ascend towards heaven.'[17]

The passage starts thus:
'I saw, in a golden beam of light,
a ladder hanging so high,
that the top remained unseen.'[18]

The illustration accompanying Well's article shows Jacob's Ladder as painted by Giovanni de Vecchi (1536-1615) and Rafaellino da Reggio (c. 1550-1578) and another by Giovanni Francesco Penni (1488-1528). In the first, three angels stand on the ladder, while in the second there are six angels. In neither case do the angels bear symbols indicating the virtues.

A further illustration of the ladder as a symbol of man's striving for perfection is found in Fludd's Utriusque Cosmi Historia,[19] which shows a six-rung ladder with the steps labeled Sensus, Imaginatio, Ratio, Intellectus, Intelligentia and Verbum, with the following explanation: 'The ladder of perfection shows the steps that must be taken to mount from Earth to Heaven: from the world of the senses to the inner world of imagination; thence through Reason, or disciplined thought, to Intellect, the inner organ of knowledge; to Intelligence, or the object of direct inner knowledge, and finally to the Word itself, which opens the super celestial realm.'

Even in present-day primitive societies, 'the belief in a ladder leading from the earth to heaven is found in several parts of the world.'[20] Examples given are the natives of Fernando Po, Timorlaut and other islands of the Indian archipelago, and the Toradjas of the Central Celebes.

It is worthy of note that the ladder symbol also continues to appear in the art of later centuries, under many different guises, but always with a spiritual connotation. Three contemporary examples will suffice. Ladders and stairways figure prominently in the works of M. C. Escher, for which various deep philosophical explanations have been advanced. The Spanish painter Joan Miro often included a ladder in his works, which he called the 'ladder of escape'. See, for instance, Dog baying to the moon' (once again, the moon symbol joined to the ladder). [21] For another, more recent example, see Anselm Kiefer's 'Resurrexit', painted in 1973. [22]

A perhaps more famous example, though not always recognized as such, is in Albrecht Durer's etching 'Melancholia I', dated 1514. This is what Frances A. Yates had to say about it: 'Melancholia's angelic character is suggested not only by her angel wings, but also by the ladder behind her, leading not to the top of the building, but generally upwards into the sky, Jacob's ladder, on which the angels ascend and descend.' [23]

The close connection of verticality, expressed by the ladder symbol, with human aspirations for spiritual perfection, and with the rites of initiation, provides us with the justification we sought for its inclusion in Masonic symbolism.

The Biblical Narrative

Since we have been dealing with Jacob's Ladder and its spiritual connections, it would be convenient to go back to the biblical origin of this image. Here is a retelling of the pertinent passages:

Jacob leaves Beersheba to go to Haran. The sun sets while he is on the way, so he decides to spend the night at a certain place, takes a stone and uses it as a pillow. During his sleep, he dreams that he sees a stairway or ladder - the Hebrew word accepts both translations - resting on the earth and reaching heaven, and angels of God ascending and descending on it. On top is God, telling Jacob that He is the Lord, God of his father Abraham and God of Isaac. God further promises Jacob to give him and his descendants the land on which he is lying, and makes other generous promises. (Genesis 28:10-13). The next morning, Jacob is struck with awe at what he had experienced, and concludes the place is holy: 'the house of God, the gate of heaven'. He takes the stone he had used as a pillow, sets it up as a pillar and pours oil on top, that is, makes it into an altar. And the Bible states that Jacob called the place Bethel ('House of God'), 'though the city used to be called Luz'.

'Luz' in all Latin-derived languages has the meaning of 'light'. Although the Hebrew name means 'almond' or 'hazelnut', as a verb it means 'to turn aside, to depart', and also 'to speak evil, to slander'. [24] This strange passage in the biblical text can then be explained as a way of saying that Jacob decides to turn aside from evil thoughts and take the first steps of ascent through the 'Gate of Heaven'.

The hazelnut is also a symbol of immortality, while according to a tradition, an almond tree stood nearby, marking the entrance to an underground city where 'the Angel of Death cannot penetrate'. [25] The Stone of Scone, also known as the Stone of Destiny, the ancient coronation seat of the kings of Scotland, is said to be that stone used as a pillow by Jacob. 'Jacob's sons supposedly carried the stone to Egypt. From there, was said to have been taken to Spain, then to Ireland where it was placed on the sacred hill at Tara.' [26]

Jacob's Ladder on the Tracing Board

The presence of Jacob's Ladder in Masonic symbolism can be explained, as we have seen, by its close connection with the mystical experience of initiation. Its representation on the Tracing Board, however, raises several questions. First, the biblical narrative mentions angels, which in the Hebrew language have the masculine gender, while our iconography (following the tradition of European painting) depicts them as females. More importantly, no connection is made in the Bible between the ascending and descending angels and the three 'theological virtues' (Faith, Hope, and Charity). These, in fact, have a distinct Christian connotation, and this runs counter to the de-Christianization of Masonic rituals and symbolism that took place early in the nineteenth century. Finally, there is an historical question, about exactly when this symbol was introduced into Freemasonry.

Let us return for a moment to the question of Jacob's Ladder as part of Masonic iconography. The relationship between altar, ladder and the heavens is spelled out in the biblical narration. The stone used as a pillow became the altar stone. The ladder on the Tracing Board rests on the altar (the stone) because Jacob's dream took place within his head, which rested there, on the stone, and the ladder reached heaven because the place was in fact the gate of heaven. The stone, then, is a link between the biblical story and the stone-builder's craft.

The Hebrew word 'soolam' can mean either a stairway or a ladder. In modern Hebrew the word is used only in its second meaning, but Bible translators have usually preferred 'stairway', while noting the possible alternative reading.

Some artists have depicted Jacob's dream with a stairway, others with a ladder. William Blake, for instance, painted a sweeping, winding stairway going through the moon into the heavens, with an indeterminate number of steps. [27] Generally, however, the number of rungs is limited, usually three or seven although other numbers have been used. [28]

An interesting explanation of the place of Jacob's Ladder in Masonic symbolism was advanced by Bro. Sir John Cockburn:

'The ladder has ever been a prominent Symbol in Masonry. It is drawn on the Tracing Boards and, as the Ladder of Perfection, it is a conspicuous object in the higher degrees of the Ancient and Accepted Rite. >From time immemorial it has been employed as the symbol of progressive ascent on the Intellectual, Moral and Spiritual planes. The number of steps varies from three upwards. The ladder reaches from Earth to Heaven and it is thus a type of the Union of the Terrestrial and Celestial Kingdoms, and of the at-one-ment between God and man, which throughout the ages has been the constant theme of the Mysteries, as well as of Philosophy and Religion.' [29]

Masonic historians, however, seem to agree that Jacob's Ladder is of relatively recent appearance as a Masonic symbol. No mention of it can be found in the oldest documentary evidence relating to our Craft. Bro. Harry Carr has written that he believes Jacob's Ladder to be 'of mid or late eighteenth century introduction, because there is no trace of it in the earlier rituals', without advancing any more precise date. [30] *Coil's Masonic Encyclopedia* proposes a date 'as late as the early nineteenth century'.

The great Masonic scholar Mackey declares that 'in the Ancient Craft degrees of the York Rite, Jacob's Ladder was not an original symbol. It is said to have been introduced by Dunckerley when he reformed the lectures. This is confirmed by the fact that it is not mentioned in any of the early rituals of the last century, nor even by Hutchinson... Its first appearance is in a tracing board on which the date of 1760 is inscribed, which very well agrees with the date of Dunckerley's improvements. In this Tracing Board, the ladder has but three rounds; a change from the old seven-stepped ladder of the mysteries - which, however, Preston corrected when he described it as having many rounds, but three principal ones.'[31]

Unfortunately, Bro. Mackey does not give more particulars about the specific Tracing Board he had in mind when writing the above, so that it cannot be now identified.

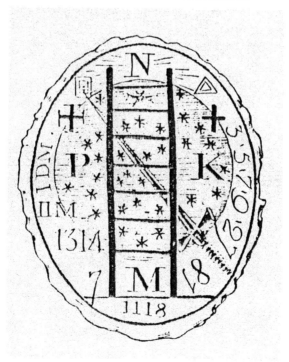

The Dunckerley Seal

Bro. Thomas Dunckerley, mentioned by Mackey, was the Provincial Grand Master in Hampshire. He was the natural son of the Prince of Wales, later King George II. He was born in 1724, initiated in 1754 and died in 1795. In his biography of Dunckerley, Bro. Henry Sadler states that 'there is a tradition that Dunckerley revised the Code of Lectures for the Craft', but he throws doubt on the truth of this idea. [32]

A theory different from that of Mackey's was advanced by Bro. G. Oliver: '... in the year 1732 Martin Clare, A.M., was commissioned to prepare a course of Lectures ... without infringing on the ancient Landmarks. These lectures were nothing more than the amplification of the system propounded by Anderson and Desaguliers, enlightened by the addition of a few moral references and ... they also contained a simple allusion to the senses, and the theological ladder - with staves or rounds innumerable'. [33]

'Martin Clare's Lectures ... were revised ... by Bro. Dunckerley, P.G.M. In these lectures Dunckerley introduced many types of Christ, and endued the ladder with three principal steps as an approach to the supernatural regions, which he called Faith, Hope and Charity. His disquisition was founded on 1 Cor. XIII, and he might have had in view the true Christian doctrine of three states of the soul.' [34]

Unfortunately, I have been unable to find documentary evidence for the above assertions. Until such proof is advanced, we shall have to take them as further examples of opinions that Bro. Oliver presented as facts.

The description of the lodge in Jachin & Boaz (1762) and in Three Distinct Knocks (1760) makes no mention of Jacob's Ladder. Neither does it appear in the early French exposures of mid-eighteenth century. [35] The plan of the Apprentice-Fellow Lodge, for instance, in L'Ordre des Francs—Macons Trahi (1745) shows numerous Masonic symbols of the first two degrees, but no ladder.

In Louis Travenol's Le Catechisme des Francs-Macons (1744) there is a plan of the Apprentice-Fellow's lodge which, in the words of the editor, constitutes the earliest known printed illustration of what ultimately became the Tracing Board. [36] There is no sign of a ladder.

W. Blake (1800)

The earliest mention (but not illustration) of Jacob's Ladder in a Masonic context that I have found appears in another work by Travenol, La Desolation des Entrepreneurs Modernes (1747) where, describing the floor drawing (also called the 'lodge') he writes: '... sometimes a Ladder is included in this Drawing, but I have never seen it in any of the Lodges I have visited and several FreeMasons, who are in the same situation as myself, claim that this Ladder is a Schism which was introduced among them by some fanatical Worshipfuls. As for me, I do not believe it. Why should not the Ladder be included among the many Ornaments or Jewels of the Lodge? ... This Ladder, which they call Jacob's Ladder, has only three rungs, which signify, so they say, the three divine virtues [notice the adjective 'divine', and not 'theological', and the distance from Heaven to Earth, or the difference between a Free-Mason and a Profane. How wonderful! After that, does anyone believe that the Worshipfuls who introduced this "commemoration" can be wrong? No, the only thing one could justly reproach them with is that they did not add to the Ladder, the rope and the scaffold, because, after all, both of them are also a part of Masonic equipment, and consequently should form part of its necessary emblems.'[37]

Disregarding Travenol's ironic double-entendre, playing with the double meaning of the word scaffold, we must conclude that here we have perhaps the earliest demonstration of the Masonic use of Jacob's Ladder, including its connection with the three Theological Virtues. However, the illustration that accompanies this description does not show the ladder.[38]

In an almost contemporary work, Le Macon Demasque (1751) there is a plate with the 'Drawing for the Apprentice-Fellow's Lodge', [39] which does not include the ladder.

There is an earlier reference, which might be construed as alluding to Jacob's Ladder, but I find it inconclusive. In an anonymous publication of 1737, we find the following passage: 'Even a faint representation of the Holy Lodge to Jacob, Gen. 28, 16 produced the Exclamation: This is none other but the House of God; this is the Gate of Heaven'. [40]

Craft Certificates, Aprons, Jewels

Another valuable source of information on the use of symbols in Masonry is Craft certificates, which often were and are embellished with symbolic drawings.

In an extensive review of English Craft certificates by Bro. T. O. Haunch,[41] there are numerous instances of the three Theological Virtues, from the early eighteenth century (Plate 9) on to 1764 (Plate 17) and until 1814 (Plate 25). The four Cardinal Virtues (Fortitude, Prudence, Justice and Temperance), portrayed as women holding a spear, a mirror, the scales or a bridle, appear in a certificate of 1766 (Plate 6). In 1821 we find all seven Virtues together (Plate 7) under the beneficent rays of the sun shining through a cloudy sky. A certificate of 1792 depicts only Faith and Hope (Plate 11). The oldest Grand Lodge certificate in the Grand Lodge collection, dated 1767, also presents the three Theological Virtues (Plate 20). However, in not even a single instance is Jacob's Ladder included in the decoration of these Masonic certificates, dating from the early eighteenth century to 1821!

The appearance of the ladder on painted or embroidered aprons can be dated to the late eighteenth century. In the Grand

Lodge Museum, in London, there are at least two aprons dated c. 1790, one showing Jacob's Ladder alone, and the other, the ladder with the initials F. H. C.

"Melencolia I" Durer, 1514

Another apron of c. 1800 shows the ladder resting on the V.S.L., and three rungs with the same initials. A further example, of the late eighteenth century, is a Dutch apron with a 3-rung ladder. [42]

Interestingly, there is a Royal Arch apron belonging to the 'Moderns' that includes a three-rung ladder joined to the image of Faith. [43]

A respected Masonic scholar has informed me that the ladder appeared in many pierced jewels of the middle or even early eighteenth century. Unfortunately, I have almost no information available on this subject and have been unable to obtain further details from other sources. A search through the collection of Ars Quatuor Coronatorum turned up only a few examples of pierced jewels, such as one of 'square and segment' type that included a seven-rung ladder of c. 1800. [44]

In his inaugural address on Masonic jewels, Bro. W.E. Heaton mentions that pierced jewels were common in the 18th century and some of the examples he brings, e.g. an Irish jewel, include a ladder. [45]

A jewel in the Grand Lodge Museum (London) dated 1776, with a miniature of Frances Cornelia, wife of W. Bro. James Ames of Wiltshire, shown on the reverse a three-rung leaning ladder.

The earliest example of something that might be a ladder, depicted in a Masonic jewel that I have found, is the Sackville medal, which dates back to 1738 or earlier. [46]

It should be underlined that in all these cases, the ladder appears alone, without any reference to the Virtues.

Early Tracing Boards

The ladder does not appear in the earliest tracing boards, as we can see in Bro. E. H. Dring's study on the subject. [47]

Let me quote some paragraphs of Dring's paper: 'Cecil Powell mentions an inventory dated 7.7.1813 on Moira Lodge of Honour N 326, which includes a Tracing Board and Green Baize cover [baize is the green felted cloth used to cover billiard and card-playing tables], plus painted tin representations of the four Cardinal Virtues, three other figures, probably the Theological Virtues, ear of corn, fall of water, J and B pillars, square, level, plumb, 24 gauge, letter G and numbers 1 to 10.' Notice that Jacob's Ladder does not appear in the list.

Another inventory, dated 24 June 1771, describes a lodge board of the Lodge of Relief N 42. Once again, the board includes many of the symbols we usually associate with the tracing board, but no mention is made of Jacob's Ladder.

Other inventories listed by Dring include even symbols that have fallen into disuse, such as the heavy maul and the bee hive, but not Jacob's Ladder.

Lodge floor cloths, an early form of the tracing board, are illustrated in Dring's article. One plate shows the lodge cloth of Silurian Lodge, dated after 1791. There is no Jacob's Ladder on it. Another lodge cloth, this of c. 1790-1800 at Kirkwall Kilwinning Lodge N 38 (Scottish Constitution) shows the two columns, sun, anchor, stairs, altar, square, crossed keys, crossed pens, hammer, level, perpendicular, mosaic pavement, candlesticks, beehive, square and compasses, triangle and winding staircase. Jacob's Ladder is not represented.

Only in later examples illustrated, dating from 1810 to 1830, does the ladder make its appearance.

The earliest tracing board in Great Britain, belonging to Faithful Lodge N 85, dated 1800, does show Jacob's Ladder, but in the 3rd degree board, not the first.

Other tracing boards, of the Lodge of Friendship N 100 (1809) and Inhabitants Lodge N 153 (1809), [48] do not include the ladder.

We must come to the conclusion that the use of Jacob's Ladder may have started around the middle of the eighteenth century, but its use did not become generalized until the beginning of the nineteenth century, more or less coinciding with the formative years of the Union (1813), at the time when the rituals used by both Grand Lodges were being compared and a unified ritual was being worked out.

In the first years after the Union, evidently, use of the ladder symbol was far from widespread. The connection between the ladder and the three Theological Virtues was also not firmly established. We have already seen the many instances of the use of the Theological Virtues with no relation to the ladder. As for the tracing boards, the board of All Souls Lodge N 170, dated 1809, has the ladder but without the Virtues. A floor cloth of Middlesex Lodge N 143, dated 1832, has the Virtues but not the ladder. Another tracing board, dated 14.4.1807, belonging to the

Plains of Mamre Preceptory, Haworth, of the Knights Templar, shows a ladder with five rungs, standing on the V.S.L., and ending in the clouds and a crown, but with no figures on it, either angels or Virtues. [49]

Anselm Kiefer "Resurrexit"

Bro. Carr notes that 'the early designs indicated the three virtues, Faith, Hope and Charity, by the initial letters F. H. and C. between the rungs; Bro. T.O. Haunch (in *A.Q.C.*, Vol. 75, pp. 190-194) believes that the initial letters came first and that Josiah Bowring, a famous designer of tracing boards, c. 1785-1830, introduced the three female figures to replace them. They appear in many tracing boards nowadays, the first holding a Bible, the second with an anchor, and the third with children nestling at her skirts.'

'Several drawings of the 1870's and later omit the figures but show a Cross, an Anchor and a Chalice with a pointing hand. Presumably the Chalice and the Hand are meant to represent Charity but they are probably illustrations of a piece of religious mythology, depicting the Holy Grail, which was snatched up to Heaven by God's Hand.' [50]

Philosophy - Notre Dame, Paris 13c.

In so far as tracing boards are concerned, Bro. Carr may be correct in his assertion but, as we have seen, female figures representing the Theological Virtues had already been used in Masonic documents long before Bowring.

Haunch explains the hand as the finger of God the Creator. Faith is represented by a cross, or by the hand of God with a finger pointing to the V.S.L., or by a chalice. Hope is represented by an anchor or a female figure holding an anchor. Charity is represented by the liberal hand extending to a chalice or a heart, or by a female figure surrounded by children. Anno Ordinus is the year according to the accounting from the foundation of the Templars Order. Used in Knight Templar documents. [51]

A serious question arises concerning the Christian nature of the three Theological Virtues, and the fact that the idea of 'ascending to heaven' is a purely religious concept, alien to the non-denominational principle guiding the founders of speculative Freemasonry. The introduction of these elements into Masonic iconography precisely at the time of the Union, when a determined attempt was made to erase all traces of Christian theology from Masonic ritual, is remarkable.

Bro. N. Barker Cryer, in his paper 'The De-Christianization of the Craft', [52] mentions several instances of Christian survivals in Masonic ritual, but does not refer specifically to Jacob's Ladder and the three Theological Virtues, which is not really surprising since, as we have seem this is not really a survival, but the introduction of a relatively new symbol.

It appears that at the time immediately before and after the Union, an effort was made by some brethren to retain or introduce Christian elements in Masonic ritual. The use of Jacob's Ladder in conjunction with the three (Christian) Theological Virtues appears to be a successful instance of this tendency.

The subsistence of some side Masonic degrees restricted to Christians - despite the unequivocal rejection of a religious qualification as a fundamental principle of Freemasonry - is another example of this attitude.

The Circular Stairway

The Tracing Board of the Second Degree in the Emulation Rite displays the circular stairway as one of its central symbols. Interestingly, Blake depicts Jacob's Ladder as a circular stairway of innumerable steps, with angels waking up and down.

The spiral or circular stairway appears in the iconography of the Tower of Babel, and in Babylonian ziggurats, as noted earlier.

In the First Book of Kings, chap. 6 verse 8, we read: 'The entrance to the middle chamber was on the south corner of the temple; a spiral stairway (in Hebrew: 'belulim') led up to the middle level and from there to the third'. The Masonic tradition is different in the various rituals. In Emulation, the Middle Chamber is the place where the Fellow Craft received their wages, while in the Scottish Rite tradition, the Middle Chamber is the meeting place of Master Masons. The circular stairway, however, supports both traditions.

The spiritual or esoteric symbolism of the circular stairway is similar to that of Jacob's Ladder, with the added significance of the steps rising in a spiral around an axis.

This is the axis mundi, another symbol linking earth and heaven.

The Kadosh Knights' Ladder

The Scottish Rite as a whole is a gradual ascent through the degrees, constituting a veritable 'mystic stairway' and an 'initiatory ladder'. The changes introduced in our rituals through the centuries have obscured, and sometimes erased, this important aspect of Freemasonry in the Craft degrees. Only the Scottish Rite, and to a lesser extent the 'higher degrees' of the York Rite, preserve elements of this esoteric tradition. The ladder represents the esoteric way towards the Major Mysteries.

The 30th Degree of the Scottish Rite (Knight Kadosh) has its central symbol the two-sided step-ladder, which seven rungs on each side. The risers or side rails make reference to biblical passages, [53] instructing the Initiate to love God and his Neighbor. The same message is repeated in the New Testament, when Jesus is asked what is the greatest commandment of all. [54]

The steps on one side of the ladder, which bear Hebrew names, represent stages of ascent to the 'Nec plus ultra', that is to say, the Absolute, or God, by whatever name He is known to the Initiate. The other side presents the names of the 'Liberal Arts' that lead to profane knowledge. The two-sided ladder thus represents both ways to reach the knowledge of the Absolute: sacred and profane.

Let us take another look at the rungs on the first side, in ascending order:

1) Tzedakah - justice, charity.

2) Shor Laban ('White bull') - innocence. It may also have reference to the constellation of Taurus. About the multiple symbolism of the color white, please refer to the chapter dealing with the symbolism of colors.

3) Matok (sweet) - pleasantness, grace.

4) Emunah (faith) - constancy, truth.

5) Amal Sagui - strenuous work. According to Philippe Van Heurck, it also refers to suffering, perseverance, great misfortune.[55]

6) Sabal - bearer of burden, endured.

7) Gmul, Binah, Tvunah - prudence. These three words, independent one from another, have various meanings:

Gmul means reward, work, good action, wages.

Binah is intelligence, comprehension.

Tvunah is intelligence, prudence, reason, wisdom, discernment.

Turning now to the other side of the ladder, again from bottom to top, we find: Grammar, Rhetoric, Logic, Arithmetic, Geometry, Music and Astronomy. There is a gradual progress from the material (grammar, rhetoric) to the abstract (logic, arithmetic, geometry) to reach the empyrean (music, astronomy-astrology).

Dante compares the seven sciences to the seven heavens.[56] The symbolism of the number seven escapes the scope of this chapter, but its importance in Freemasonry cannot be ignored.

In many old illustrations, the two-sided ladder is capped by the two-headed eagle. This image of spirit as composed of two distinct elements (since the eagle, as we know, is a symbol of the spirit) is reflected in another name of the Knight Kadosh: he is Knight of the Black and White Eagle.

The symbolic ascent and descent of the Initiate over the two-sided ladder represents a mystic journey, or pilgrimage. Thus, it makes reference to the labyrinth and some passages of the initiation ceremony in the Ancient and Accepted Scottish Rite.

A different explanation of the seven-step ladder, and its connection with the Templars Order, which is another important element in the 30th degree tradition, concerns the seal on a Knight Templar's certificate, known as the Dunckerley Seal.[57]

The explanation given by Bro. J. Knight, is believed to have been copied from a document supplied by Dunckerley himself:

'The Ladder with Seven Steps or rounds alludes to the Seven Degrees of Masonry; the letter M at the foot of the Ladder implies Masonry; the letter N at the top, the Ne plus Ultra of the Science. The N 1118 at the bottom, denotes the date of Origin of the [Templars] Order, which being deducted from the Current year, gives the Anno Ordinus.[58] The 11 M - 1314 on the Dexter Side denotes the Martyrdom of J[acques] D[e] M[olay], the Grand Master of the Order, which being deducted from the current Year, gives the Anno Caedus [Year of the Immolation. De Molay was executed on 11 March 1314 CE]. The letters P on the Dexter and K on the Sinister side of the Ladder denotes that the Order originated in Palestine, and was preserved at Kilwinning. The initials I.D.M. denotes I.D.M. [Jacques De Molay] as before mentioned. The figures 3, 5, 7, 9, 27, 81, on the Sinister Side are the Masonic Numbers, or the different Ages of a Man in Masonry [to each of the 33 degrees of the AASR corresponds a symbolic age].'

The seal represents a clear link between the traditions of the higher degrees of the York Rite and those of the Scottish Rite.

Chapter Notes

1 R. W. Carroll & Co, Publishers, Cincinnati, 1872. Reprinted by The Masonic Book Club, Vol. 28, 1997.
2 Henderson, Joseph L. and Oakes, Maud, The Wisdom of the Serpent, Collier, New York 1971, p. 268 and Plate 25.
3 Guerillot, Claude, 'La Symbolique des Echelles Mystiques', Ordo ab Chao (Supreme Council of France), N 41, First Semester 2000, p. 10.
4 Coil's Masonic Encyclopedia, Macoy, New York, sub voc. Jacob's Ladder; Theological Ladder. For an illustration and

explanation of the ten Sephirot, see Purce, Jill, The Mystic Spiral, Thames and Hudson, London, 1980, pp. 108-109.
5 Lenhof, Eugene and Posner, Oskar, Internationales Freimaurerlexicon, Vienna, 1932, reprinted 1980, sub voc. Leiter (p. 911
6 Seiffert, Oskar, Dictionary of Classical Antiquities, Meridian Books, 1956, sub voc. Horus (pp. 308-309)
7 Eliade, Mircea, Images et Symboles. I have used the Spanish translation published by Taurus, Madrid, 1955, p. 51.
8 Henderson & Oakes, op cit., pp. 46-47.
9 Katzenellenbogen, Adolf, Allegories of the Virtues and Vices in Mediaeval Art, London, The Warburg Institute, 1939, p. 22.
10 Jung, Carl G., 'Dream Symbols of the Individuation Process', in Campbell, ed. Spiritual Disciplines, p. 350, quoted in Henderson and Oakes
11 Cf. the 'Fraternal' or 'Union Chain' which in Continental working serves to close every masonic ceremony. This is also symbolized by the knotted rope that encircles some lodge rooms.
12 Wells, Robin Headlam, 'The Ladder of Love', Early Music Journal, Vol. 12, N 2, Oxford, May 1984, pp. 173-189.
13 Wells, Robin Headlam, 'The Ladder of Love', Early Music Journal, Vol. 12, N 2, Oxford, May 1984, pp. 173-189.
14 Farre, Jean, Dictionary of Masonic Symbols, Editions du Rocher, 1997. Spanish translation Kompas Ediciones, Madrid, 1998, p. 130.
15 Wells, op. cit. p. 178.
16 Gúrillot, op. cit., p. 11.
17 I am indebted to Bro. N. B. Cryer for bringing this work to my attention. Hilton's work is abundantly quoted in Evelyn Underhill's Mysticism, Meridian Books, New York 1955, where the most recent editions (at the time) of Hilton's books are also listed.
18 Wells, op. cit., p. 180.
19 Divine Comedy, Paradiso, Canto 21, lines 28-30.
20 Fludd, Robert, Tomus Secundus De Supernaturali, Naturali, Praeternaturali Et Contranaturali Microcosmos Historia, in Tractatus Tres Distributa, Oppenheim, Johanmn

Theodore de Bry, 1619, p. 272, reproduced in Godwyn, Joscelyn, Robert Fludd, Thames and Hudson, London 1979, p. 71. The quotation explaining the ladder has been taken from the same source.

21 Gaster, Theodor H., Myth, Legend and Custom in the Old Testament, Harper & Row, New York. I have available only the Spanish translation, published by Barral, Barcelona, 1971, pp. 239-240.

22 Gaster, Theodor H., Myth, Legend and Custom in the Old Testament, Harper & Row, New York. I have available only the Spanish translation, published by Barral, Barcelona, 1971, pp. 239-240.

23 Reproduced in Cook, Roger, The Tree of Life, Avon, New York 1974, plate 62.

24 Reproduced in Newsweek, 9 December 1985, p. 55.

25 Yates, Frances A., The Occult Philosophy in the Elizabethan Age, Routledge and Kegan Paul, London 1979, p. 56.

26 Klein, Ernest, A Comprehensive Etymological Dictionary of the Hebrew Language for Readers of English, Carta, Jerusalem 1987, p. 296.

27 Bizzarri, Mariano, 'La Scala Misteriosa nel XXX grado del Rito Scozzese', Massoneria Oggi, Roma, January-February 1997, p. 15.

28 English to give back Stone of Scone, 700 years later', The Jerusalem Post, 4 July 1996.

29 Reproduced in Purce, Jill, The Mystic Spiral, Thames and Hudson, London 1980, plate 45.

30 See, e.g., 'Der Traum Jakobs' by Adam Elsheimer (1578-1610), Frankfurt Museum of Art, Cat. N 2136, showing the ladder and three winged angels. An earlier representation, dating from c. 1160, is in an illuminated parchment in the Kupferstichkabinett Berlin-Dahlem (MS 78AG fol. 4v), reproduced in Suchal, Fran(ois, Art of the Early Middle Ages, Abrams, New York 1968. Another early illustration, from the Aelferic Paraphrase of the Heptateuch, an eleventh century manuscript (London, Broting Museum Cotton MS. CLAUD B. IV;vol. 44v) is reproduced in Encyclopedia Judaica, Vol., 9, p. 1193, fig. 1.

31 Cockburn, Sir John, The Symbolism of Jacob's Ladder, Wallasey, 1925, p.3.
32 Carr, Harry, The Freemason at Work, London 1976, p. 117.
33 ackey, Albert, An Encyclopedia of Freemasonry, New York and London, 1913, sub voc. Jacob's Ladder, p. 361.
34 Sadler, Henry, Thomas Dunckerley. His life, labours and letters, London 1891, pp. 14 and 224.
35 Sadler, Henry, Thomas Dunckerley. His life, labours and letters, London 1891, pp. 14 and 224.
36 Oliver, G., The Symbol of Glory, New York 1855, p. 58.
37 Oliver, op. cit., p. 59
38 Carr, Harry, ed., Early French Exposures, London 1971, p. 243.
39 Carr, E.F.E., p. 95.
40 Carr, E.F.E., p. 338.
41 Carr, E.F.E., p. 337.
42 Carr, E.F.E., p. 441.
43 Anon, On Scripture Masonry, London 1737, p. 13, reproduced in Grand Lodge Library N 19670, B. 86 Sel.
43 Haunch, T.O., 'English Craft Certificates', A.Q.C. 82 (1969), p. 169 et seq.
44 A.Q.C., VI (1893), p. 160.
45 A.Q.C., V (1892), p. 31
46 A.Q.C. 83 (1970), p. 113.
47 A.Q.C. 60 (1947), pp. 201-204.
48 A.Q.C. XII (1899), p. 204.
49 Dring, E. H., 'The Evolution and Development of the Tracing or Lodge Board', A.Q.C. 29 (1916), pp. 243-265 and 275-297.
50 Pictured in A.Q.C. 13, p. 37.
51 A.Q.C. 23 (1910), p. 164.
52 Carr, The Freemason at Work, p. 118.
53 Haunch, T.O., 'The First Tracing Board', A.Q.C., 84 (1971), pp. 326-328.
54 A.Q.C. , 97 (1984), pp. 33-74.
55 Deuteronomy 5:6: 'Love the Lord your God with all your heart and with all your soul and with all your strength', and Leviticus 19:18: 'Love your neighbor as yourself.'

56 Matthew 22:34-40.
57 Quoted by Raoul Berteaux, Le Rite Ecossais Ancien et Accept*, EDIMAF, Paris 1987, pp. 190-191.
58 Convivio, v. II, chap. XIV. Quoted by Mariano Bizzarri, 'La Scala Misteriosa nel XXX grado del Rito Scozzese', Massoneria Oggi, Roma, January-February 1997, p. 12.
59 'Notes and Queries', Ars Quatuor Coronatorum, Vol. 18 (1905), p. 43.
60 Anno Ordinus is the year according to the accounting from the foundation of the Templars Order. Used in Knight Templar documents.

Chapter 4

COLOR SYMBOLISM IN FREEMASONRY

Introduction

Color is a fundamental component of Masonic symbolism. It appears in the descriptions of aprons, sashes and other items of regalia, in the furnishings and wall-hangings of the lodge room for each degree or ceremony, in the robes worn in certain degrees, and in many other Masonic accoutrements. The colors specified in each case appear to have no rational explanation. As A. E. Waite wrote: 'There is no recognized scheme or science of colors in Masonry'.[1] Here and there in our rituals we find an 'explanation' for the use of a certain color, but this usually turns out to be merely a peg on which to hang a homiletic lecture about it, having little if any connection with the origins of its use.

In this chapter we shall try to find some rationale behind the selection of colors as Masonic symbols, restricting our examination to the Craft degrees, and those of the Ancient and Accepted Scottish Rite, with occasional reference to the Royal Arch.[2] No attempt will be made to deal exhaustively with all the symbolic meanings attached to each hue. The task would be immense, and is unnecessary for our purpose.[3] We shall, therefore, limit ourselves to that symbolism that has a direct bearing on Freemasonry. If an exception is made here and there, it just proves that all rules are made to be broken! Symbolism is a tricky subject, where one can very easily find whatever one is looking for in the first place. My conclusions should be taken with a healthy measure of skepticism, and they are of course subject to review as newer or different evidence is presented.

Color And Symbolism

It was early recognized that colors have a strong influence on the mind and, therefore, can be employed for certain moral or aesthetic ends, through symbolical, allegorical and mystical allusions. Newton wrote of 'the sensual and moral effects of color', [4] where the word sensual must be understood as 'transmitted by the senses'. Goethe, too, wrote extensively on color (over 2,000 pages!).

The Accepted Theories

We can profitably start our discussion by quoting the introduction to the chapter on 'Masonic Colours and their Symbolism' in Bro. Bernard E. Jones authoritative Masonic handbook: [5]

Colours have so large a place in the customs of the Craft that inevitably the question arises: Did ancient symbolism inspire the colours of Masonry, or were they first chosen and the symbolism then found to fit them? Many years ago a writer who went deeply into the question came to the conclusion that the English Grand Lodge, in choosing the colours of its clothing, was guided mainly by the colours associated with the Noble Orders of the Garter and the Bath. This idea is more or less confirmed by the late Henry Sadler, an authority universally respected, who said: 'Having looked at the matter from every conceivable point of view, I have failed to think of a more favorable explanation'. We must conclude, therefore, that Freemasonry's colours were no more derived from ancient symbolism than were the colours of the liturgical vestments of the Christian Church from those of the Jewish priests.

The clothing of three groups of degrees is related mainly to three colours: the Craft or symbolic degrees with blue; the Royal Arch with crimson; and the allied degrees with green, white and other colours, including black. F. J. W. Crowe has suggested that the deep-blue color - the Oxford blue - of the Grand Officers' clothing was borrowed from the ribbon of the Most Noble Order of the Garter. When the 'Garter' was instituted... about 1348...

its color was light blue, but soon after the accession of George I, in 1714, this light blue was changed to the present deep blue to distinguish the color of the Order from that which the Stuarts in banishment on the Continent had conferred on their adherents. As for the light blue - Cambridge blue - of private lodge clothing, this was deliberately chosen to contrast with, and mark the difference from, the deep blue of Grand Lodge clothing.

The Grand Stewards' crimson, [Crowe] suggests, was take from the Most Honorable Order of the Bath, revived by George I in 1725... The Scottish Grand Lodge took its green ('thistle' green) from that of the Most Ancient and Most Noble Order of the Thistle, restored by James VII and II in 1687 and re-established by Queen Anne in 1703.

The Grand Lodge of Ireland chose its light blue probably with the object of making a contrast to that of the dark blue of the English Grand Lodge, and in so doing anticipated the light blue of the Most Illustrious Order of St. Patrick, founded for Ireland by George III in 1783 and revised in 1905.

As we shall see later, I have found some strong arguments to dispute these conclusions.

Masonic Blue

Blue, then is the Craft color par excellence, used in aprons, collars, and elsewhere. Let me quote Bro. Chetwode Crawley: **6** 'The ordinary prosaic enquirer will see in the selection of blue as the distinctive color of Freemasonry only the natural sequence of the legend of King Solomon's Temple. For the Jews had been Divinely commanded to wear... a "riband of blue" (Numbers 15:38)'.

However, a modern translation of that verse in Numbers is: 'You are to take tassels on the corners of your garments with a blue cord in each tassel'. The biblical text, therefore, refers only to blue cords to be incorporated in the tassels worn by pious Jews, while Bro. Chetwode Crawley speaks of blue ribbons which somehow became the embellishments of aprons, sashes and collars. His attribution appears to be poorly founded.

Another suggested source of the color blue mentioned by Bro. Chetwode Crawley could be its association with St. Mary, mother of Jesus, 'so prominent a figure in the pre-Reformation invocations of the Old Charges, drawing in her train the red ensign of St. George of Cappadocia, her steward and our Patron Saint'. In fact, many medieval and later paintings depict St. Mary wearing a blue gown or cloak.

Blue and red, the heraldic azure and gules, are sometimes associated with the chevron of the Arms of the Masons' Company. I shall deal later with the symbolism of white, blue, red and the other colors used in Freemasonry. For the time being, let us continue our historical examination.

Use Of Color In The Grand Lodge Of England

There can be little doubt that operative masons wore undecorated white aprons. Many old paintings and illustrations demonstrate this fact. [7] The banner of the Masons' Guild of Strasbourg in the fourth century depicts three black hammers in a 'bend' (a diagonal band running from upper left to lower right of the shield) on a white background. [8]

At first the premier Grand Lodge continued this operative tradition. A Grand Lodge resolution of 24 June 1727 orders the Worshipful Master and Wardens of all private lodges to wear 'the jewels of Masonry hanging to a white ribbon...' Crowe points out that in 'the engraved portrait of Anthony Sayer, the first Grand Master of the Grand Lodge of 1717, copied from a painting by Joseph Highmore, the apron is certainly plain white without any addition, thus showing the absence of color to be universal for all ranks. This is the earliest known representation of our apron.' [9]

This situation, however, changed rapidly. In the Grand Lodge Minutes of 17 March 1731 we read that 'The Grand Master, his Deputy and Wardens shall wear their Jewels in Gold or Gilt pendant to blue Ribbons about their necks, and white leather Aprons lined with blue silk'. The same applied to past Grand Officers. As for Stewards and Past Stewards, they would wear aprons lined with red silk and red ribbons. Curiously, the principal Officers of the private lodges would continue wearing plain white regalia.

As for the exact shade of blue intended, we can learn from the Rawlinson MS (C. 136) of 1734 that the blue of the Grand Master's apron is characterized as garter blue, as is the Deputy Grand Master's. 'We may assume, therefore, that the Ribbons and apron-linings of Grand Officers were blue in colours from 1727 onwards ... On the authority of the Memorandum of 1734, we can take it as assured that the recognized color of Grand Officers; clothing had by that time become garter blue'. [10] So says Bro. Chetwode Crawley. He then goes into the history of the color called garter blue, the color of the ribbon used for the Order of the Garter. 'In the early days of the Order ... all authorities concur in depicting it as a very pale blue ... till the Tudor period. The blue of the Order lost its watery tinge and became a light sky-blue, a hue which it retained until the Hanoverian period. [11] Eventually the hue was deepened to what is now known as garter blue, and our immediate object is to determine as exactly as possible the time at which the change occurred.' His conclusion is that the change took place about 1745.

The Grand Lodge of Ireland, which was the first to introduce the custom of constituting lodges by means of Charters or Warrants, used ribbons in a pale shade of sky-blue to attach the seals to the early warrants (1730-1). This, too, has been taken as proof that the color used by the brethren in those early days was light blue. It has also been suggested that this shade takes its origin from the Irish flag: 'Azure, a harp or'. [12]

The Choice Of Masonic Colors

As already observed, the use of the term 'garter blue' has led Masonic scholars to believe that this color was chosen with the Order of the Garter in mind as a matter of prestige. Bro. Bernard E. Jones, quoted above, expounds this theory proposed by Crowe, who when discussing the color adopted by the Grand Lodge of Ireland claims that it 'anticipated the formation of the Most Illustrious Order of St. Patrick in 1788 by selecting light blue.' [13] However, not a shred of evidence exists to support Crowe's opinion. In fact, the notion that our Irish brethren could somehow anticipate the color to be chosen fifty years later for a new order of knighthood is but an extreme example of the tendency to bend the facts to make them fit with a preconceived idea.

That 'garter blue' was prescribed in 1734 does not in itself establish a link with the chivalric Order. The specification of colors has always been a perplexing subject, and the use of examples to serve as description has long been customary: sea blue, sky blue, teal blue, apple green, bottle green, olive green, daffodil yellow, Bordeaux red, charcoal gray are a few instances. Only with the invention of the spectroscope (1859) was the scientific analysis of color made possible; still, only in the 20th century the shades of dyes used in the textile industry began to be specified scientifically.

Therefore, stating that 'garter blue' should be used is simply using 'garter' as a descriptive term and must not be taken as demonstrating that the selection was inspired by a desire to create a link with the Order of the Garter. In this connection, it is significant that Bernard Jones, discussing the color of the Grand Officers' clothing, calls it Oxford blue, and that for private lodges Cambridge blue. [14] Are we to conclude from this that Craft degrees of Masonry have some connection with the two great universities? Of course not. 'Oxford', 'Cambridge' and 'garter' are all being used as examples to describe the color.

It has been also suggested that Past Grand Officers' jewels are similar in shape to the 'Lesser George' (one of the items of regalia in the Order of the Garter) which is pendent from a sash over the left shoulder, as in the Royal Arch. This, however, is mere speculation. Ceremonial sashes are often so worn to distinguish them from the baldric (which can be used to support a sword). 'Jewels' (in the sense of insignia, Masonic or otherwise) tend to be circular or oval in form, for ease of manufacture and because they hang well.

Chetwode Crawley dismisses the conjecture that the use of red in the Royal Arch was adopted from the ribbon of the Order of the Bath: '[This] can hardly be considered tenable ... for the Order of the Bath was subordinate ... and far inferior in popular estimation [to that of the Garter]'. His argument appears to be that the color of a lesser Order of Knighthood would not be conferred on the holder of a superior

Masonic degree. Another brother has suggested that the two colors of the Royal Arch are those of the livery of the Hanoverian royal family,[15] that of the Royal Arch first appears to have been crimson alone. [16]

As for the green used in Scottish Grand Lodge regalia, Crowe believes that 'there can be no doubt that the green of the Order of the Thistle as deliberately selected'. But he further informs us that 'In Scotland aprons are found of every shade, and even combination, of red, blue, white, green and tartan ... the colours in use in private lodges are not even permanent, but appear to be changed at pleasure.'

In Scotland, as in England, aprons were at first white. They are mentioned in lodge records shortly after the middle of the seventeenth century. Only in 1736, when the Grand Lodge was formed, was green selected. However, as Robert Lindsay notes in his History of the Lodge of Holyrood House (St Luke's) N : 44 [17] 'Grand Lodge did not produce its first set of jewels and clothing until 30th November 1765, and, therefore, it had no occasion to use its color before this date. Green without a difference is now forbidden as a color to any subordinate Scottish Lodge'. If green had been chosen for Grand Officers to reflect the Order of the Thistle, it would have been logical for all lodges to use it rather than to allow almost complete freedom of choice.

Classification Of Colors Under Different Masonic Constitutions

Crowe offers as a classification:

First - Those which confine themselves to various shades of blue. This comprises most Grand Lodges.

Second - Craft lodges working under 'Grand Orients' which generally replace blue by red, both in the apron and in lodge decorations. Exceptions are the Grand United Lusitanian Orient of Portugal (light blue and gold, similar to Ireland) and the Grand Orient of Belgium (blue silk, edged and embroidered with gold).

Third - Those, such as Scotland and the Netherlands, in which each subordinate lodge can choose its own color.

Fourth - The Grand Lodge of Egypt [long since defunct], which replaced blue with dark and light green.

The Grand Orient of Italy, he thought, represented a special case; using green to adorn the Fellow Craft apron, while a Master Mason's was trimmed in red and accompanied by a green sash. Crowe suggests that the use of green could have been due to the influence of a Scottish Jacobite lodge working in Rome in 1735. In Egypt the use of green could have been due to Italian influence.

I would point out that green is a color traditionally connected with Islam and would be a natural choice for Egyptian regalia. As for the Italian's preference for green, this may be explained by the use of the name VERDI as a motto during the struggle to establish a constitutional monarchy in Italy. Verdi (which means 'green' in the plural), apart from being the name of the great composer, are the initials of Vittorio Emmanuele Re D'Italia.

The Masonic Symbolism Of Colors

White

White, the original color of the Masonic apron, and still universally used for the aprons of Entered Apprentices, was always considered an emblem of purity and innocence, exemplified in images such as the white lily or fallen snow.

Even today, some Grand Lodges (e.g. Washington D.C.) prescribe white aprons for all its brethren, whatever may be their Masonic rank. Aprons including colors other than white usually have the color as a border around the edges and as lining, preserving white for its center field.

Plato [18] asserts that white is par excellence the color of the gods. In the Bible, Daniel sees God as a very old man, dressed in robes white as snow (Daniel 7:9). In the New Testament Jesus is transfigured on Mount Tabor before Peter, James and John, when his clothes became 'dazzling white, whiter than anyone in the world could bleach them (Mark 9:3). Officiating priests of many religions wore and still wear white garments. In ancient

Jerusalem both the priests (Cohanim) and the Levites who performed the Temple rites assumed white clothing.

Wilhelm I of Prussia
Painting in the Deutsches Freimaur Museum, Bayreuth

Among Romans, the unblemished character of the person aspiring to public office was indicated by a toga whitened with chalk. This is the origin of the word 'candidate', from candidatus, 'dressed in white'. Verdicts at trials were decided by small stones (calculi) thrown into an urn: white to absolve, black to condemn.[19] This custom is preserved in Masonic lodges using white and black balls for balloting a candidate for initiation. White signifies beginnings, virtualities, the white page facing the writer, 'the space where the possible may become reality'. [20] White is, therefore, understandably the color of initiation. It is a symbol of perfection, as represented by the swan in the legend of Lohengrin. [21] In this aspect it is related to light or the sky blue, which in Hebrew is tchelet and is connected semantically with tichlah (perfection, completeness) and tachlit (completeness, purpose).[22] (See also the observations on the symbolism of blue, below). Among the Celts the sacred colors of white, blue and green were understood to stand for light, truth and hope. [23] Druids also were white robes.

White is also connected with the idea of death and resurrection. Shrouds are white; spirits are represented as wearing white veils. White, rather than black, is sometimes the color of mourning, among the ancient kings of France, for instance, and in Japan. [24]

White, finally, can signify joy. Leukos (Greek) means both white and cheerful, as does candidus in Latin. The Romans marked festive days with lime (white) and unlucky days with charcoal.

Blue

Blue is the color of the canopy of heaven: azure, cerulean or sky blue. 'Universally, it denotes immortality, eternity, chastity, fidelity; pale blue, in particular, represents prudence and goodness". [25] In the Royal Arch, the Third Principal is told that it is an emblem of beneficence and charity.

In biblical times, blue was closely related to purple. Generations of scholars have puzzled over the correct meaning of tchelet (light blue) and argaman (purple), often mentioned together, without reaching a satisfactory explanation. Only recently has the problem been finally solved in the course of far-reaching research into the dyestuffs and dyeing methods used by the ancient Phoenicians and Hebrews. Both hues, it turns out, were produced with dyestuffs extracted from murex, a shellfish abundant on the coast of Lebanon. The tchelet was obtained from a short-spined variety (murex trunculus), while the argaman came from two kinds: the single-spined murex brandaris and, to a lesser extent, the Red-mouth (thais haemastoma). [26]

Some historians have concluded that, in the Middle Ages in Europe, blue was low in popular esteem. The favorite color was red because the dyers could achieve strong shades of it, which brought to mind the prestigious purple of the ancient world. Towards the end of that period, blue gradually became recognized as a princely color, the 'Royal Blue' which displaced red at court, red then being used by the lower classes and so regarded as vulgar. Blue and gold (or yellow) then became the colors of choice for shields, banners and livery. [27]

It may not be by chance, therefore, that the Master was said to be clothed in 'yellow jacket and blue breeches' in the famous metaphor first used in the exposure 'The Mystery of Freemasonry', that appeared in The Daily Journal in 1730. [28] The traditional explanation of the phrase relates it to the compasses, its arms of gold, gilt or brass, and the points of steel or iron. However, while steel can certainly appear bluish, iron cannot!

Blue was used royally in France, noticeably as the background to the fleur-de-lys. It became associated with terms of prestige such as blue blood, cordon bleu (originally the sash of the Order of the Holy Spirit), blue riband (of the Atlantic), and blue chip.

Purple

Purple is a symbol of imperial royalty and richness, but can also relate to penitence and the solemnity of Lent and the Advent in the seasons of the Christian church. Although described (in the Royal Arch, for instance) as 'an emblem of union, being composed of blue and crimson', I believe this to be a somewhat contrived explanation. An interesting fact, which appears to have escaped the attention of most writers on this subject, is that in the Cabala, the Hebrew word for purple, argaman, is a mnemonic, representing the initials of the names of the five principal angels in Jewish esotericism (Uriel, Raphael, Gabriel, Michael and Nuriel).

Red

Red or crimson, the color of fire and heat, is traditionally associated with war and the military. In Rome, the paludamentum, the robe worn by generals, was red in color. The color of blood is naturally connected with the idea of sacrifice, struggle and heroism. It also denotes charity, devotion, abnegation - perhaps recalling the pelican that feeds its progeny with its own blood.

In Hebrew, the name of the first man, Adam, is akin to red, blood and earth (adom, dam and adamah, respectively). This connection with earth may explain, perhaps, the connection of red with the passions, carnal love, the cosmetics used by women to attract their lovers. It is the color of youth. Generally, it represents expansive force and vitality. It is the emblem of faith and fortitude and, in the Royal Arch, of fervency and zeal. Red has also a darker side, connected with the flames of hell, the appearance of demons, the apoplectic face of rage. [29] Scarlet was the distinctive color of the Order of the Golden Fleece, established in 1429 by Philip the Good, Duke of Burgundy (1419-67). Not only was the mantle scarlet, but also the robe and a special hat - the chaperon - with hanging streamers. [30]

Green

'Green has been directly associated with the ideas of resurrection and immortality. The acacia (the Masonic green) has been suggested as a symbol of a moral life or rebirth, and also of immortality. To the ancient Egyptians, green was the symbol of hope.'[31]

As already noted, the Grand Lodge of Scotland has adopted green as its emblematic color, and, in varying degrees, it is incorporated in the dress and furnishings of degrees and Orders beyond the Craft in English, Scottish and Irish Freemasonry.

Yellow

Yellow is rarely used in Masonic regalia, except in some higher degrees. It is an ambivalent color, representing the best and the worst, the color of brass and honey, but also of sulfur and cowardice. Yellow is the perfection of the Golden Age, the priceless quality of the Golden Fleece and the golden apples of the Hesperides. It is also the color of the patch imposed on the Jews as a badge of infamy. In the sixteenth century, the door of a traitor's home was painted yellow. [32] A 'jaundiced view' expressed hostility, but the most memorable symbolism of yellow is that it reminds us of the sun and of gold.

Black

The three fundamental colors found in all civilizations, down to the Middle Ages in Europe, are white, red and black. These, too, may be regarded as the principal colors of Freemasonry: the white of the Craft degrees, the red of the Royal Arch and of certain degrees of the Ancient and Accepted Scottish Rite, and the black of some of its others, and of the Knights of Malta. The other colors of the rainbow find limited uses; they serve only to frame or line the white lambskin upon which so many aprons are based, or for sashes and other items of regalia.

Traditionally, black is the color of darkness, death, the underworld, although it was not introduced for mourning until about the middle of the fourteenth century, [33] such use becoming habitual only in the sixteenth. The 'black humor' of melancholy (atara bilis), the black crow of ill omen, the black mass, black market, 'black days': all refer to negative aspects. The Black Stone at Mecca is believed by Muslims to have been at one time white; the sins of man caused the transformation.

Black has also positive aspects, those of gravity and sobriety; the Reformation in Europe frowned upon colorful clothing. Formal dress for day and evening wear continues to be mostly black. Religious Jews dress in black as do many Christian sects. Black is also associated with the outlaw and the banner of pirates and anarchists, but also with birth and transformation (it's the first stage of alchemical work: the nigredo).

In the French and Scottish Rites, the lodge in the third degree is decorated in black and is strewn with white or silver tears, representing the sorrow caused by the death of Hiram Abif.

Heraldic Colors

Since many Masonic degrees have a chivalric background, it is not irrelevant to provide here some information about the symbolic allusions of the colors used in heraldry.

The heraldic colors are seven, corresponding to the seven planets known in antiquity (which included the sun and the moon). Two are 'metals': or and argent (gold and silver), usually represented by yellow and white; the others are called 'enamels', 'tinctures' or simply colors: sable, gules, azure, vert or sinople, and purpure (black, red, blue, green and purple). The last-named, being considered a synthesis of the others, is regarded both as a metal and an enamel. [34]

Heraldic tinctures have metaphysical significance, differentiating them from ordinary colors. Classification into 'metals' and 'enamels' brings to mind working with fire, a transmutation from physical to spiritual light centering on gold, the alchemical work.

Jean Vassel [35] writes that 'the transmutation from yellow into gold symbolizes the transformation of refracted and indirect conscience to immediate and direct conscience'. This operation is one of the aspects of the alchemical 'manufacture of gold'. On this basis, the use of heraldic colors is governed by rules which derive their significance from the alchemical stages of the Great Work.

The hierarchy of colors 'expresses effectively different stages of being'. [36] This would be the reason for the fundamental rule of heraldic art: neither metal above metal nor enamel above enamel.[37] The most notable exception to this rule if the gold on silver in the Arms of Jerusalem, explained by the fact that the Holy City is the connecting point between heaven and earth.

The symbolism attached to each heraldic color may be summarized thus:

Argent (white): rebirth, initiation. Its lunar shade represents crossing waters, baptism, the first discovery of light.

Sable (black): death. Originally, neither a tincture nor a metal, but rather a fur (zibeline) which changes its skin color going from black to white and from white to black. This changing of the skin may refer to the three initiatic deaths.

Gules (red): war, combat, sacrifice, courage.

Azure (blue): the heavens, cosmic mastery, unity, passage from earth to heaven.

Or (gold): center of spiritual life, passage from the minor to the major mysteries. Through gold the terrestrial knight transmutes himself into the celestial knight.

Vert (green): new life, immortality, the Holy Grail.

Purpure (purple): climax of the hermetic scale, the thrice-potent gods (Hermes, Mercury and Toth), the philosopher's stone, the plenitude of spirit and imperial sovereignty over the universe.

Conclusion

A review of the traditional 'explanations' for the choice of certain colors in Masonic symbolism reveals their weaknesses. In considering the use of blue in the English regalia of a Master Mason, it has been possible to find a connection between the Hebrew language, the Bible, and other reasons for its choice.

The symbolism of the colors used in the various degrees of the Ancient and Accepted Scottish Rite will be the subject of the next chapter.

Acknowledgments

I am grateful for the help given by Bro. Frederick Seal-Coon, Bro. John Hamill (at the time Librarian at Freemasons' Hall, London), the editors of El Mercurio newspaper of Santiago, Chile, and the staff of the Iowa Masonic Library in collecting the material for this chapter.

Chapter Notes

1 Waite, Arthur Edward, A New Encyclopaedia of Freemasonry, London 1921, vol. 1, p. 113.
2 I am aware of the many doubts about the provenance of the qualification 'Scottish' in this context. However, with the

exception of the Supreme Councils of England, Scotland, Ireland, Finland and Australia, all regard themselves as governing the Ancient and Accepted Scottish Rite and, in America, the term 'Scottish Rite' is a well-understood colloquialism.

3 A useful introduction to the general symbolism of colors is the work by Fredric Portal, Des Couleurs Symboliques, Guy Trdaniel, Paris 1979 (reprinted 1984). This is not a scientific work, but it is very complete.

4 Quoted by Rypprecht Matthaei (ed.), Goethe's Colour Theory, Studio Vista, London 1971, p. 168.

5 Jones, Bernard E., Freemasons' Guide and Compendium, Harrap, London 1950, p. 470.

6 Chetwode Crawley, W.J., 'Masonic Blue', AQC 23 (1910), pp. 309-20.

7 See, for example, the famous illustration of the reception of mason 'compagnons' by the Grand Master of the Order of Hospitallers of St. John of Jerusalem, at the siege of Rhodes, c. 1480, taken from MS Latin 6067, fol. 9 Vo, of the National Library of Paris. The only worker with an apron, on the extreme right, is wearing a white apron. This picture was reproduced in color on the cover of Humanisme, April 1990, N. 190.

8 See illustration and details in 'Guild Banners', Ciba Review, N 77, Basle, December 1949, p. 2819.

9 Crowe, F. J. W, 'Colours in Freemasonry', AQC 17 (1904), p. 3.

10 Chetwode Crawley, op. cit., p. 312.

11 The Order of the Garter was created in 1346-8. The Tudor period extends from 1485 to 1603. The Hanoverian period starts in 1714.

12 Oliver, Andrew, 'Colours in Freemasonry', AQC 17 (1904), p. 176.

13 Crowe, op. cit., pp. 110-111.

14 Jones, op. cit., p. 470.

15 Gordon Hills, commenting on Bro. Crowe's paper, op. cit., p. 9.

16 Bro. W. H. Rylands, commenting on Bro. Crowe's paper,

op. cit., p. 10.
17 Edinburgh 1935, p. 137.
18 The Laws, XII, 956a. Quoted by Mension-Rigau. See note 20.
19 Mentioned by Ovid, The Metamorphoses, 15, 41-2.

20 Mension-Rigau, Eric, 'Historia del Color - III - El Blanco: Donde lo Posible puede ser Realidad', El Mercurio, Santiago, Chile, 3 February 1991.
21 Ibid.
22 Klein, Ernst, A Comprehensive Etymological Dictionary of the Hebrew Language for Readers of English, Carta, Jerusalem, 1987.
23 Crowe, op. cit., p. 110.
24 Mension-Rigau, op. cit.
25 Jones, op. cit., p. 471.
26 Ron, Moshe, 'Tchelet and Argaman' (in Hebrew), Yalkut, N 103, Jerusalem, September 1984, p. 19 and Ziderman, Israel, 'The difference between Tchelet and Argaman' (in Hebrew), Yalkut, N 104, Jerusalem, January 1985, p. 38.
27 Mension-Rigau, 'La Mansedumbre del Azul', El Mercurio, Santiago, Chile, 9 December 1990.
28 Carr, Henry, The Freemason at Work, London, 7th ed. 1992, p. 5. The newspaper exposure was actually preceded by a reference to 'yellow and blue, meaning the compass, which is brass and iron' in the Dumfries N 4 MS of c. 1710.
29 Mension-Rigau, 'Dejemos hablar al Rojo', El Mercurio, Santiago, Chile, 13 January 1991.
30 Wescher, H., 'Fabrics and Colours in the Ceremonial of the Court of Burgundy', Ciba Review, N 51, Basle, July 1946, p. 1851.
31 Jones, op. cit., p. 472.
32 Mension-Rigau, 'El Amarillo - S.mbolo de lo Mejor y lol Mercurio, Santiago, Chile, 24 February 1991.
33 Mension-Rigau, 'Melancol.a, Encierro y Austeridad del Negro', El Mercurio, Santiago, Chile, 10 March 1991.

34 Most of the information in this section has been taken from Grard de Serval, 'Introduction a l'tude du langage symbolique du blason', Travaux de la Loge Nationale de Recherches Villard de Honnecourt, N 3 (2nd series), (2nd semester of 1981), pp. 17-43.
35 Le symbolisme des Couleurs Heraldiques', Etudes Traditionelles, 1950.
36 De Serval, op. cit., p. 23.
37 'One of the earliest rules one learns in the study of armory is that colour cannot be placed upon colour, nor metal upon metal. Now this is a definite rule which must practically always be rigidly observed. Many writers have gone so far as to say that the only case of an infraction of this rule will be found in the arms of Jerusalem: Argent, a cross potent between two crosslets or.' A. C. Fox-Davies, A Complete Guide to Heraldry, New York 1978, p. 85.

Chapter 5

THE SYMBOLISM OF COLORS IN THE ANCIENT AND ACCEPTED SCOTTISH RITE

Introduction

In this chapter we shall study the main colors specified in the liturgy of each Scottish Rite degree, taking into consideration their symbolic and traditional meaning, as well as their psychological and historical significance.

In most degrees, the color of the Lodge Room - that is the color of the walls or the hangings that cover them - is specified for each part of the ceremony. These have been listed in the synoptic tables below under 'Temple'.

Other colors of importance in each degree are those of the regalia - apron, sash, collar, gloves, etc. Some degrees involve wearing robes or capes. Their color is noted, as well as that of the lining in some cases. These have been designated as 'cloaks' in the tables below, while secondary colors (used for the lining, edging, decorations) are enclosed within parentheses. Sometimes, the collar is replaced by a ribbon or sash worn diagonally over one shoulder. In these cases, the indication "R" (ribbon) has been added.

Essentially, we have considered the colors indicated by Paul Naudon en his extensive work on the history and symbolism of the Scottish Rite degrees, [1] confronting his indications with those appearing illustrated in *A Bridge to Light* by Rex R. Hutchens [2], who based his choice of colors on those indicated in Albert Pike's works, particularly *Morals and Dogma* and his Liturgy for the various degrees. When both sources disagree, both are noted, marking Naudon's description with an (N) and Hutchen's with an (H).

Psychological And Historical Background

In order to understand the reasons for the choice of one color or another in our rituals, we must first learn something of the psychological and historical symbolism attached to each color in Western civilization. The remarks below constitute only a few signposts, hints for further study. A full investigation of the symbolic significance of all the colors figuring in Masonic rituals would fill several volumes. I shall add a few specific comments at appropriate places, when discussing each individual degree.

Further information on the Masonic symbolism of color can be found, inter alia, in the following: Bernard E. Jones, *Freemason's Guide and Companion*, G.L. Harrap, London, 1950, pp. 470-473, and F.J.W. Crowe, '*Colours in Freemasonry*', AQC 17 (1904), pp. 3-11, as well as the preceding chapter in this book, which also contains a useful bibliography.

White is the color of light and of beginnings, the world of possibilities, the blank page before the writer, the canvas awaiting the painter's touch of color. It also represents innocence ('Candor' comes from the Latin word for white).

Black is the shade of night, mourning, the interior of the earth, the tomb, absence of light, the opposite of white. Though associated with death (in Western civilization, at least), it has its positive aspects. It's the color of germination, of the darkest moment of the night before dawn's light bursts forth, of simplicity and seriousness of purpose.

Red is the primary color, the color of fire, heat, life, enthusiasm ... and danger. It is the only color that becomes stronger when saturated. All others lose brilliance. Red expands in all directions, representing the sublimation of matter, intelligence, affection.

The three above hues are the fundamental colors in alchemical symbolism, denoting successive stages of the alchemical transformation ("work"). Alchemy influenced strongly various degrees that eventually became part of the Scottish Rite scale.

Blue is the color of water and sky, life, motherhood, eternity, the heavens. Of all colors, it's the most relaxing one. While red speaks of matter, blue refers to spirit. Red is action and blue, contemplation. Blue represents what is exalted and ethereal in nature.

After these preliminary explanations, let us now examine the symbolism of the colors used in the various Scottish Rite degrees, in their sequence.

First Class

Following the division proposed by Naudon (p. 299) we shall study the colors of the different degrees classified into seven progressive classes.

Generally, the division is not arbitrary, but corresponds to the origins of each group of degrees, which eventually became integrated within the Scottish Rite system.

The first class comprises the three traditional symbolic or craft degrees: Entered Apprentice, Fellow-Craft and Master Mason.

In the Scottish Rite, both Entered Apprentice and Fellow-Craft wear a plain white apron (however, they wear it differently, either in the position of the flap or tucking a corner), while the apron of a Master Mason is white edged in red and lined in black. I must stress that we are dealing exclusively with the colors used in the Scottish Rite. These are not the aprons customary in the United States, where blue is habitually used for craft degrees. The manner of wearing the apron and even the shape may differ from one Jurisdiction to another. However, what I state concerning Scottish Rite aprons is valid for many Grand Lodges in Europe and Latin-America, where the Scottish Rite is worked in all degrees, including the first three.

The Lodge Room is blue in the two first degrees, and black in the third. Gloves are white in all three.

The three colors in these degrees, white, black and red, are also the three fundamental shades in the psychology of colors. In reality, white and black are not properly colors, rather they denote the presence or absence of light, respectively. Sometimes, they are called "achromatic" or, in plain English, colorless colors.

White light comprises lights of all colors (this is known as an additive mixture of colors), while the mixture of all pigments or paints - theoretically, at least - should produce black (this is known as a subtractive mixture).

Red, on its own, is the color par excellence. In some primitive tribes, the only color that has a specific name is red.

In the Hebrew language, the same word root (aleph-daleth-mem) appears in the words meaning 'red', 'man' and 'earth'.

Second Class

The second class comprises the degrees 4 to 8. These are the first degrees in the Lodge of Perfection, and they share a common thread in their legendary stories, related to the punishment of Hiram's murderers, the reward given for services rendered, the search for a replacement for Hiram and the completion of the Temple, including the building of a secret vault. Another main symbolic component is the search for the lost Master's word.

	COLORS OF THE DEGREES 4 TO 8				
	4th	5th	6th	7th	8th
Temple	Black	Green (white)	Black (white tears)	Red	Crimson*
Apron	White (black/blue)	White (green)	White (red)	White (red)	White (red/green)
Collar	(N)Blue(black) (H) White (black)	Green-R	Crimson-R	Crimson-R	Crimson-R
Gloves	(N) Black (H) White(black)	White			
*Crimson is a deep purplish red.					

The repeated appearance of white as the main color of the apron is remarkable. This fact underlines the continuity of these degrees with respect to the symbolic degrees. Secondary colors are related to the legend of each degree. Thus, black (in the 4) reminds us that mourning still observed in this degree (tomb of H.A., loss of the word), while blue represents Faith (Q: What is the characteristic of the fourth degree? A: It's an act of faith).

The black Temple represents the Sanctum Sanctorum of King Solomon's Temple. The master's jewel is a golden triangle (or three triangles). Gold - represented graphically by yellow - is symbolic of wisdom.

The legend of the 5 is related to the creation of the universe (green). This color also reflects the motive of death-resurrection. It may also refer to the Password of the degree, which is an evergreen.

White (5) is related to beginnings and perfection.

The combination of red and crimson of the 6 degree suggests an excess of zeal, which is explained in detail in the legend of the degree.

Envy, which figures prominently in the legend of the 7, is symbolized by the red Temple and the crimson ribbon.

The green decoration of the 8 again refers to the idea of creation (construction).

Third Class

The third class comprises the three degrees from the 9 to the 11. These are the so-called degrees of vengeance, or of the Elect Ones (Elus), because the main theme in their legends is that of vengeance for the terrible crime of the bad Companions, and the punishment they suffered thereafter. These degrees form a distinct group and, according to some historians of our Rite, they are chronologically the oldest "Scottish" degrees, created in the first half of the 18th century.

COLORS OF THE DEGREES 9TH TO 11TH		
9th	**10th**	**11th**
Temple Black (red/white)	Black (red/white)	Black (red/white)
Apron White (red/black)	White (black)	White (blac/red)
Collar Black (red)	Black - R	Black (red) - R
Gloves Black	Black	Black

The predominant color in these degrees is black, representing sorrow, ignorance and error, while the scarlet of zeal and vengeance appears as a secondary color. The white aprons serve to maintain continuity with the previous degrees, and also demonstrate the innocence of those wearing them.

Fourth Class

The fourth class, 12 to 14, which also have reference to the 7 and 8 degrees, are connected with construction and architecture, particularly the sacred vault under the Holy of Holies.

COLORS OF THE DEGREES 12TH TO 14TH		
	12th	13th	14th
Temple	White (scarlet *)	Black (white)	Crimson (white)
Apron	White (blue/gold)	(N) None (H) Crimson	White (crimson/blue)
Cloak		**	
Collar	Blue - R	Purple - R	Crimson (green)
Gloves		(H) Black	

* Scarlet is a bright red.
** Albert Pike, in his Liturgy prescribes a yellow robe for the presiding officer, and a chasuble of crimson satin lined with blue. The Warden wears a purple robe and the Inspector, a white robe, both without the chasuble.

The Temple, as we can appreciate, is decorated successively with the three principal Masonic colors that we have noted before (white, black, red). The apron continues to be white.

The collars, when taking the three degrees together, remind us of the three colors of the Royal Arch. This should not surprise us, since the Royal Arch legend also appears in these degrees, although in a form slightly different from that known in Royal Arch masonry.

Fifth Class

The fifth class comprises the so-called "Chapter" or Rose - Croix degrees, from the 15 to the 18. The majority of these degrees require two or more rooms to execute in full form their ceremonies, each decorated in a distinctive and equally important color. Of these degrees, the first, 'Knight of the East', 'of the Sword' or 'of the Eagle', is very old, being a further development beyond the Lodge of Perfection. The Temple in these degrees is no longer that of Solomon, but rather that built by Zerubabel upon the return of the Jews from their Babylonian exile.

	COLORS OF THE DEGREES 15 TO 18			
	15th	16th	17th	18th
Temple	1-Green 2- Crimson *	(N)1-Golden Yellow 2- Red (H)Green	Scarlet	1-Black (white) 2-Black 3-Scarlet
Apron	(N) White (green) (H) Crimson (Green)	Crimson (H) (saffron) (N) (Golden Yellow)	Yellow (crimson)	White(black, crimson)
Sash	(H) White (gold)			
Robe			(N) White	
Collar	Green - R	Saffron - R (N) Golden Yellow	White-Black-R	(N)Red(black R (H) R-Black-Crimson
Gloves	(N) White (H) Green	(H)Scarlet	Black	White
Hat	(H) Black (green)			

* There are two separate rooms in this degree.

The dominant color in these degrees is red. The golden yellow (in French it is called 'color of the dawn') in the 16th degree is perhaps a reference to the symbolic hour for opening the Chapter. Question: At what time do the Princes of Jerusalem rise and fight? Answer: When the sun rises above the horizon.

The numerous references to gold in this degree are better understood in connection with its name: Prince of Jerusalem. The heraldic colors of the Holy City are gold and silver. Furthermore, there are numerous literary references to King Solomon's capital city as "Golden Jerusalem".

Sixth Class

The sixth class comprises the degrees 19 to 27. These are called the Philosophical Degrees. For convenience, we shall study them divided into three groups comprising three degrees each. This division is arbitrary, and has no symbolic significance.

	COLORS OF THE DEGREES 19 TO 21		
	19th	20th	21st
Temple	Blue (gold)	Blue (gold)	Silver
Apron	none	(N) none (H) Yellow (sky-blue)	Yellow
Cloak	White		
Collar	Crimson (white/gold)-R	Yellow (sky-blue)-R	Black
Gloves		Yellow	(N) Black (H) Yellow
Headband	Blue	none	none

The Temple in these degrees (except the 21st degree) is Blue, alluding to Heavenly Jerusalem and the reconstruction of the Holy City.

The yellow appearing in the 20th degree may be explained by the fact that the recipient of this degree is awarded the title of Very Respectable Grand Master of all Symbolic Lodges. Gold, represented graphically by yellow, is related to the center, wisdom, nobility and geometry.

The 21st Degree constitutes an exception in many ways. Firstly, the use of yellow for the apron. This deviation from white had been observed before in the 17th degree. Both degrees, in fact, stand apart from the central line of Masonic legends and have nothing to do with the construction of Jerusalem's Temple, neither that of King Solomon, nor that of Ezra-Nehemiah.

The silver color of the lodge room represents in reality the light of the moon, which in this degree is supposed to constitute the room's only illumination.

COLORS OF THE DEGREES 22 TO 24			
	22nd	23rd	24th
Temple	Blue - Red	White (red/black)	Black
Apron	White (purple)	(N) none (H) White (scarlet/red/blue/purple)	(N) White (flame red) (H) White (scarlet/light green)
Cloak		Red-White (yellow/gold/black/silver)	Blue
Collar	Rainbow (red) (H) (purple)	None	Scarlet (gold)-R
Gloves		Blue	White
Belt		(H) Red	(H) Light green

Let us now examine the colors of the degrees 23 to 27. These five degrees were inserted into the 25 degrees of the old Rite of Perfection in order to create the present Ancient and Accepted Scottish Rite of 33 degrees. They were apparently taken from the Order of Trinitarian Scotsmen.

Many colors are repeated from previous degrees, and their explanation should be found above. An interesting deviation is the use of blue for the gloves in the 23 Degree (Chief of the Tabernacle). Possibly, this alludes to the clothing of the Grand Priest in the Temple of Jerusalem, which was almost totally blue. Some authors indicate that the cloak used in this degree should also be blue, instead of the colors appearing in the tables.

COLORS OF THE DEGREES 25 TO 27			
	25th	26th	27th
Temple	Red (H) Red-Blue	Green (white/red)	Red (black)
Apron	(N) none (H) White (black, gold)	Scarlet (H) (white, Sky-blue) (N) (White, Green)	Scarlet (black, white)
Cloak		(H) Green, White, Red	White (red)
Collar	Crimson-White-R	(H) Green, White, Red-R	White (red)
Gloves			(N) White (red) (H) White, Red, Black

Seventh Class

These six degrees are the culmination of the Scottish system. The first three are related to the Kadosh degree (Knight Kadosh), one of the fundamental 'Scottish' degrees which served for a time as the highest degree of the canon preceding the AASR.

COLORS OF THE DEGREES 28 TO 30			
	28th	29th	30th
Temple	Landscapes	(N) Red (white) (H) Green (gold)	Black/White/Blue/Red (*) (H) Red-Black
Cloak	Red (Golden yellow, green)	Scarlet	White (black)
Apron	(N) none (H) White (vermillion)	none	none Black sash
Collar	White (gold)	(N) Crimson (H) Green (crimson) + white scarf	Black(sliver/red)
Gloves	White	Black	(N) Black or none (H) White

* The colors of the four chambers of the Temple and that of the cloak are taken from Raoul Berteaux, Le Rite Ecossais

Ancien et Accept? (15 - 33), Editions EDIMAF, Paris, 1987, pp. 193-194.

In these degrees no apron is used. The use of black gloves in the 29th and 30th degrees contrasts with the white gloves used in the next three degrees. They are related, of course, to the theme of death and vengeance of the Kadosh.

Administrative Degrees

The last three degrees are known as Administrative Degrees, although this is not entirely correct, since the 32, Master (or Prince) of the Royal Secret, presents the entire Scottish Rite scale of degrees in a coherent and logical system.

Again, in these degrees the apron is no longer used, perhaps to indicate that when reaching this level of development, the Mason no longer works physically, but only intellectually.

COLORS OF THE DEGREES 31 TO 33			
	31st	32nd	33rd
Temple	White (gold)	Black (silver)	Purple(green/white/red)
Apron	(N) none (H) none or white*	(N) none (H) White(black) (scarlet)	none
Collar	(N) Black (H) White	Black (silver/crimson)	White (gold)
Sash		(N) Black (silver/red) (H) Red - Black	White(gold)
Gloves	White	White	White

* Used only in the past, when visiting lower degrees.
See Rex. R. Hutchens, op. cit. p. 297.

The use of purple for the 33rd degree is remarkable. Purple is the color both of the Emperor and the Pope. White and Gold (or yellow) are likewise the colors of the Vatican flag. Yellow, in masonic symbolism, represents wisdom,[3] which is undoubtedly appropriate for the last and most illustrious degree of the Scottish Rite.

Summary

We have concluded our examination of the color symbolism contained in the 33 degrees of the Scottish Rite. As all symbols appearing in Masonic rituals, the colors have been chosen with a purpose in mind and are not the result of a chance or arbitrary decision.

Traditional and psychological symbolisms have been used, but perhaps what is most evident is the recurring motive of Rosicrucian-alchemical symbolism. This is not surprising when taking into account the close connections existing between early Freemasons and Rosicrucianism. Bro. A.C.F. Jackson has examined this aspect in his Rose Croix (1980). [4]

While blue is without question the fundamental color of British Craft Freemasonry, the alchemical colors: red (crimson), black and white, are the mainstay of Scottish Rite color symbolism. Green, too, appears frequently, as a sign of life, regeneration and rebirth. Gold, or its graphic representation, yellow, is often used, symbolizing light, the sun, and similar concepts.

We have only scratched the surface of the rich symbolism contained in our rituals and legendary tales. However, it is my hope that by reflecting on the above explanations, every Mason will gain a richer understanding of the rituals he observes, and may draw added pleasure and insight from his participation in the ceremonies of our Order.

Chapter Notes

[1] Historire, Rituels et Tuileur des Hauts Grades Maconniques, Dervy-Livres, Fourth Edition, Paris 1984.
[2] Hutchens, Rex R., 32 KCCH, A Bridge to Light, Supreme Council 33, AASR of Freemasonry, Southern Jurisdiction, U.S.A., 1988.
[3] Mantz, Elmer, Ph.D., 'The Symbolic Colors', New York Masonic Outlook , March 1926, p.204.

4 See also the same author's paper on 'Rosicrucianism and its effect on Craft Masonry', AQC, Vol. 97 (1984), pp. 115-133

Chapter 6

THE LABYRINTH

Introduction

The labyrinth is a symbolic design that, as we shall see, has connection with the initiation and other esoteric motives related to Freemasonry.

The idea of a labyrinth is probably associated to the cavern or grotto. The cavern, claim many ethnographers, constituted in antiquity the link between the world of the living and the land of the dead. The candidate to the Mysteries went through the initiation trials within the "initiatory cavern," and then came out as a new man. Initiation, as we know, represents a rite of death and rebirth. The idea of the "Mother Earth" is also related to these concepts, since the exit from the cavern is symbolically equivalent to childbirth. When the neophyte comes out, he is born to a new life.

Fig. 1

Concerning the etymology of the word labyrinth, Paul de Saint-Hilaire wrote that the syllable "lab" reminds us of "labor," that is, effort, work. In Latin, the name of the labyrinth is "laborintus," which underlines the relation (Schaub). Furthermore, "labor" is a synonym for childbirth.

Mircea Eliade advances another etymology, deriving it from the Asian word labra/laura, the cave, the stone, the grotto (Ragosin).

Labyrinths are widespread, appearing in coins (Fig. 1), inscriptions and buildings since antiquity and until the 17th century.

The oldest known labyrinth was found in Egypt, built near lake Moeris by pharaoh Amenemhe III (12th dynasty). According to Herodotus, it surpassed in beauty the temples of Ephesus and Samos, contained three thousand chambers, some at ground level, some others above and others yet underground.

Fig. 2

The Cretan Labyrinth

The most famous labyrinth, without doubt, is the Cretan, connected with the name of the architect Daedalus who built that labyrinth for king Minos in Cnossos, capital of Crete. That is the location of the legend of Theseus, Ariadne and the Minotaur. In labyrinths of the ancient world, the images of Theseus and the Minotaur often appeared in their center (Fig. 2). This image also appears in coins dating from the 5th to 1st centuries BCE, represented either in square or round shape. The path was single, leading from the circumference to the center, but changing direction from time to time, forcing the walker to turn many times.

This type of labyrinth represents the initiating path, since whoever comes in cannot stray aside. Consequently, this is not really a labyrinth, but rather a tortuous path.

The Labyrinth in churches

Henri Leclercq, in his dictionary of archeology and Christian Liturgy, explains that if the labyrinth was to offer various options, all of them except one leading to blind alleys, that would contradict Christian doctrine, because it would mean that the believer could err in his road in search of the Kingdom of Heaven (Schaub, p. 141). Therefore, church labyrinths have only a single path.

In labyrinths built in Christian churches, the motive of Theseus and the Minotaur disappears. In one of the year 380 (church of Saint Reparato, near Orleansville in Algeria) in the center appear the words Sancta Ecclesia (Holy Church) repeated several times (Fig. 3).

Fig. 3

Labyrinths continue appearing in Roman times and later in the Middle Ages. In cathedrals and other sacred buildings, the labyrinth is generally a design made of tiles or mosaic embedded in the floor.

In France, the labyrinths of the 12th and 13th centuries were generally known as "the road to Jerusalem" or "the league." Other designations were "the house of Daedalus," "Solomon's labyrinth" or "Solomon's prison."

The labyrinth in the floor of a church represented symbolically the pilgrimage road to Jerusalem, the Holy City. At the time of the Crusades and the building of cathedrals, pilgrims who for some reason could not make the exhausting and perilous journey to Palestine, made a symbolic pilgrimage traveling round the labyrinth on their knees. The course lasted generally one hour, equivalent to the time it took to walk one league (about 3 miles or 5.5 kilometers). For this reason, labyrinths were also known as "the league" (I. Deschamps, quoted in Schaub, p. 142) (Fig. 4).

Fig. 4

As for the appellation "Solomon's labyrinth," this refers to Cabalistic traditions. Some labyrinths shaped like a cross are known in Italy as "Solomon's knot" (Cirlot, p. 174).

The shape of the labyrinth can be circular or square (Fig. 5), exceptionally octagonal, as in the cathedrals of Reims and Amiens (Fig. 6), but more often it is circular, formed by concentric circles of the "road." Its size can reach over 12 meters in diameter, like that of Chartres, for instance (Fig. 7).

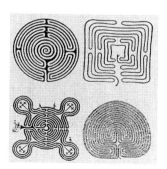

Fig 5

According to some traditions, the Compagnons (members of a French craftsmen's fraternity), each time they visited a church, they went in through a special door and walked a circular course inside the church, which they called "the small labyrinth" (Pierrier, p. 151).

Another interpretation for the reason why labyrinths were introduced in medieval cathedrals appears in the Hindu Sthapataya-veda (literally "knowledge of establishment"). According to that text, the shape of the labyrinth neutralizes the negative forces (gargoyles and other decorative elements), acting as a kind of trap. In this manner, the spiritual building residence of the divinity can be erected.

Fig. 6

Mazes, open-air labyrinths with walls made of hedgerows, were popular in England in Elizabethan and Stuart times. Hedge mazes were a common feature in gardens. Julian's Bower is one of the few remaining turf mazes in Britain. It was first recorded in 1697 but its real origin is unknown. The symbolism of the mazes is the same as that of labyrinths.

Symbolism

Probably, the use of labyrinths inside the cathedrals represented symbolically the course of human life, full of obstacles, reverses and returns.

The labyrinth, with its tortuous course from which one cannot escape, represents the Kingdom of Death. The labyrinth is at the same time the terrestrial world, the place of mystery, of initiation, where one dies and is reborn in the process of metamorphosis to become a new person.

The labyrinth in the Church of San Vitale, in Ravenna, dating from the 6th century, indicates the exit of the labyrinth (rebirth) with arrows pointing out from the center.

Fig. 7

Another idea with respect to the symbolism of the labyrinth relates it to the Via Crucis, or Way of the Cross, the path taken by Jesus from Pilate's house to Calvary.

Louis Charpentier, in his book The Mysteries of Chartres Cathedral (Laffont, 1966) mentions another possibility, which is that whoever traverses its circular path, concentrates in his person the tellurian force of the sacred place, the same as an induction bobbin (Ragusin, p. 144).

The mandala, a sacramental symbolic design in circular shape, constitutes a sacred space that helps to conduct the person meditating to illumination. He concentrates his attention in the center of the mandala (equivalent to the center of the labyrinth). Buddhist monks draw mandalas with colored sands, and then walk over the drawings erasing them. Again, we find the connection between the circle and walking. Somewhat similar designs are drawn by American Indians.

C.G. Jung makes use of the mandala image to designate a symbolic representation of the psyche.

The labyrinth, as a place of initiation, points out the return to the origin, the womb. Coming out of the labyrinth after having reached the center is equivalent to a rebirth. Santarcangeli proposes that the labyrinth, being an image of man's journey to death and rebirth, is a representation of infinity.

Beresniak mentions Fulcanelli's opinion, relating the single-path labyrinth with the alchemical work; the labyrinth expresses the two great difficulties faced by alchemical work: one, to reach the inner chamber, and two, having the possibility of coming out.

An interesting development is the fashionable "rebirth" of labyrinths in the United States, Europe and Australia, where a hundred have been built in churches, hospitals, universities and other public buildings. Lauren Artress, a priest in Grace Cathedral of San Francisco, conducts a world campaign to create labyrinths everywhere. She maintains an Internet site (www.gracecom.org) with information about contemporary labyrinths.

The Theosophical Society of America has a "meditative labyrinth" in the grounds of its headquarters in Wheaton, Minnesota.

Michel Cugnet refers to the esoteric interpretation of the labyrinth. The traveler, after overcoming the obstacles of the tortuous road, which represents the dangers of profane life, reaches the center, the interior of the cavern or womb, where the image of the deepest ego is hidden in the darkness of the unconscious. Then, when coming out, he takes this image to daylight, in order to acquire full consciousness, the knowledge of himself.

In the Minotaur legend, entrance to the labyrinth represents descent to hell, the cavern where the darkness of the unconscious is dominant. One cannot reach the depth of the unconscious except by strenuous effort, great concentration, and after advancing and going back many times. Once reaching the center, the unconscious, its awful nature is revealed, in the shape of a monster that must be conquered. Theseus, son of king Egeos or the god Poseidon, is who must kill the monster, the Minotaur with human body and head of a bull (image of mindless power).

The Minotaur was the child of Pasiphae (king Minos's wife) and a bull. By defeating the Minotaur, Theseus acquires real power over Athens, that is, acquires self-knowledge. However, to achieve this objective, Theseus must come out of the labyrinth, with the help of the leading thread given by Ariadne, daughter of Minos and half-sister of the Minotaur. Ariadne, as the muse of poets and artists, inspires the hero and plays the role of what the psychologist C.G. Jung calls the "anima," that is, the feminine aspect of the unconscious.

After giving to Theseus the key or thread leading to knowledge, Ariadne must disappear. That is why Theseus abandons her in the island of Naxos, after having acquired full self-knowledge.

Consequently, it is not sufficient to reach the center of the labyrinth, but it is necessary to go out in order to fulfill the Great Work.

Masonic symbolism

In an initiation ritual of the Lodge in Avignon, of the year 1774, the candidate is conducted in three "mysterious voyages," circulating around the room.

At the conclusion of the first circumambulation, the Junior Warden says: "This is a gentleman who wants to follow the path of virtue."

The Worshipful Master replies: "He is not on the right way, let him retrace his steps."

At the end of the second symbolic voyage, the Junior Warden says: "This is a gentleman who continues following the path of virtue."

The candidate is again led back.

After the third round, it is said: "Finally it is a gentleman who perseveres in the path of virtue." Then the Master responds: "He has followed a good road, let us hope he can arrive."

The connection with the symbolic pilgrimage on a labyrinth is quite clear. Similar procedure is followed in the initiation ritual of the Ancient and Accepted Scottish Rite.

In another section of the Scottish Rite initiation ritual, the candidate, still hoodwinked, is led out of the lodge room and made to follow a tortuous path for some moments, before returning. Then, when coming back into the lodge room, he must bend down, as if passing through a narrow entrance, perhaps the entrance to a cavern, or a symbol of coming out of the womb in delivery.

The same idea of esoteric journey appears often in Masonic rituals, presented under different shapes. The various steps when entering the lodge room, different in each degree (also called "marches"), is an example. Circumambulating is another.

The labyrinth represents for the Mason his slow progress within Freemasonry, with apparent reversals, but finally reaching the center, that is to say, self-knowledge.

Bibliography

Beresniak, Daniel, Le Labyrinthe Image du Monde, Detrad, 1996.
Cirlot, Juan Eduardo, Dicionario de Sombolos (English translation: A Dictionary of Symbols, Dorset Press, 1991).
Cugnet, Michel, " Une forme de voyage initiatique", Alpina, Swiss Masonic Journal, 5/1999, p. 152.
Di Franco, "Il giardino dei Barbarigo", Officinae, 12/1996.
Pierrier, "Une image du chemin de la vie", Alpina, Swiss Masonic Journal, 5/1999, p. 150.
Ragusin, Luc, "Le labyrinthe un et multiple", Alpina, Swiss Masonic Journal, 5/1999, p. 144.
Santarcangeli, Paolo, Il libro dei Labirinti, Frassinelli, 1984.
Schaub, Orazio, "Come mai, I labirinti nelle cattedrali?", Alpina, Swiss Masonic Journal, 5/1999, p. 140.

Chapter 7

SAINTS JOHN, SOLSTICES AND FREEMASONRY

In many countries, Freemasons follow an ancient tradition and celebrate twice a year, the so-called Solsticial Feasts, also known as Festivities of St. John, the Evangelist in December and the Baptist in June.

It is well known that the inclination of the earth's axis in relation with the plane of its orbit around the sun originates an apparent upward and downward movement of the sun. That is, during six months the sun rises and sets at points on the horizon a little to the south of those of the previous day, while in the other six months of the year, the movement is reversed and the sun slowly ascends toward the north. This is the cause for the changing seasons. The dates when the sun stops moving in one direction and reverses its apparent course are called solstices (from the Latin for 'sun' and 'stop'). The winter solstice, in the northern hemisphere, falls between December 21 and 22, and marks the sun's lowest point above the horizon. It is as if the sun was approaching death, and in many cultures special ceremonies were performed, destined to prevent the continued descent of the sun, ensuring its rebirth, that is, the beginning of its northward journey. To this effect, fires of different kinds were lit, sometimes accompanied by human sacrifices. Possibly the Jewish 'feast of lights', Hanukah, held in December, as well as the lights on the Christmas tree, have their origin in ceremonies of this kind.

Freemasons, however, do not celebrate solstices for astronomical reasons, nor in remembrance of a pagan rite. Our purpose is both more elevated and more involved. It is important to understand it, for in these celebrations much of Masonic philosophy is expressed.

The invariable course of the planets in heaven, the eternal cycle of yearly solstices and equinoxes (annus, the year in Latin, is related to the word for circle or ring, the anulus), constitute the most striking demonstration of the order that reigns in Nature.

This order, however, must reflect an act of creation. Ordo ab Chao. In other words, the act of creation itself is a process of introducing order. The Book of Genesis makes this very clear, God 'separates' light from darkness, water from water (sky and earth), the day from the night.

Let me add a few more examples to expand on this concept. Let us imagine an artist, holding a palette with all the colors he intends to use. All the colors are there. But as long as the painter does not impose a certain order, placing dab after dab of color upon the canvas, the colors remain an incoherent collection of pigments. Only owing to the order imposed by the artist is the work of art born.

Take another example. Should we imagine an orchestra, the best in the world, where we instruct the musicians to play each according to his heart's content, what would be the result? An intolerable cacophony! Only through the order established by the composer and interpreted by the conductor and the players, are the sounds of the instruments transformed into music.

The genetic code of the human species has been deciphered. The 'Human Genome' has been published, with all its 30 or 40 thousand genes. All that makes us human, from the color of the eyes, hair and skin to height, intelligence and inherited diseases, all of them are determined by the order of four basic elements arranged along the double helix of the DNA: adenine, guanine, cytosine and thymine. I repeat, the chemical composition of the genetic code is invariable, only the order of these four bases introduces all the enormous differences between one individual and another.

A last example, our English alphabet is composed of 26 letters. Other alphabets have a few more letters, or a few less. The point is, with less than thirty graphic signs we can represent all of world literature, philosophy and history. What distinguishes one idea from another, one word from the others, is simply the order in which the letters are placed.

Order, then, lies at the base of reason, logic, all sciences, all creation. That is why we represent the divinity in our Order (note the name!) as the Great Architect of the Universe. The great builder who introduces order in place of chaos. Disorder is the law of madness. A disordered mind is the antithesis of reason.

Let us return for a moment to the alphabet. Assume that all of Shakespeare's works comprise a million letters. It makes no difference for our example if the number is not accurate. Assume, also, that we have a computer program that selects letters and spaces at random and sends them to the printer. According to the laws of probability, at a certain point the computer would print the entire works of Shakespeare in the right order. Fine, but any reader who has elementary knowledge of statistics will appreciate at once that the number of permutations involved are so huge that we have no way of expressing the time required to perform them. [1]

Random combinations, then, could not have produced Shakespeare's works. The work of one writer, a few books among the many thousands or millions that have been written. What shall we say, then, of the permutations required for designing a cell, a living organism, a human being? How many aleatory - chance - combinations would result in the atoms and molecules that compose the millions upon millions of galaxies and stars dispersed in the universe? Is that really a rational hypothesis?

In my opinion, order in the universe is the irrefutable evidence that a superior reason does exist, inscrutable for us, which we designate the Great Architect. That is why we celebrate the solstices, in homage to the immutable order of nature that reminds us, day after day, year after year, that our lives must not be left to the rule of chance, the law of madness, but to that of order, reason, the logic of mathematics, the queen of sciences, represented in our Temples by the letter G placed in the center of the Lodge.

Everything else in our institution arises from that fundamental premise. Tolerance, fraternity, equality, are but partial aspects of the inevitable conclusion that a well-formed soul must draw before the stupendous spectacle of a world ruled by order.

Order is the mark of the Mason. Order in his manner of standing, walking, speaking, in the course of the ritual. Do we not say that a Lodge is regular when it is truly Masonic? Regular means following a rule, an order.

Order, moreover, implies something else. It implies an objective, an end. The work of art if born when the artist orders the colors in order to achieve a certain result. Words are ordered by the writer or the poet to express his ideas.

If all creation implies introducing order, and all ordering implies an objective, our world is not a theater of the absurd, but the expression of an intention, an objective which we may be unable to conceive or explain, but which must necessarily exist because of the very fact that the world is in order and not in chaos.

1 For those who are curious, taking a space as an additional character, the number of permutations would be 27 raised to the millionth power:

Chapter 8

THE OPENING RITUAL

Masonic ritual should be studied on three levels. First, the obvious meaning of the text and the procedures to be followed in Lodge. This might be designated as the exoteric meaning of the ritual. Second, the symbolic meaning of expressions, terms and signs, also including the symbolism of the Temple decoration and of the regalia. Finally, the 'esoteric' level which, to be able to understand, we must study it in the light of the mystical, philosophical and esoteric doctrines known to those brethren who formulated and perfected our rituals, starting centuries ago.

The Opening Ritual, although very simple and brief in comparison with the rituals of initiation, passing and raising, has a deep philosophical meaning, not always well understood. Sometimes we even hear criticism, implied if not outspoken, about the time wasted in the opening ritual, about its repetitive nature and the intransigent adherence to fixed formulas it demands.

The explanations that follow are intended to demonstrate the need for the Opening Ritual, which marks the transition from the secular world to the sacramental or consecrated world embodied in the Lodge. Without this transition no true Masonic work would be possible.

Recent research [1] shows that ritual behavior elicits brain states that bring on feelings ranging from mild community to deep spiritual unity. Rituals also tend to focus the mind, blocking out sensory perceptions.

Personal Participation

The first words of the Worshipful Master in opening the Lodge, are to request the assistance of all brethren for this purpose. It is not enough for the Master to announce that the Lodge is open. Every one of those present must feel personally involved in the proceedings that are to begin.

Freemasonry is a communal enterprise. This fact is stressed later, when describing the number of Officers that must be present to open the Lodge. The Lodge cannot function properly with less than seven Masons present.

As we have already noted, opening the Lodge implies a break with the profane, separating the Masonic consecrated space and time from the secular world outside. This separation is mental, rather than physical.

The Lodge, let us remember, is not only the room where brethren meet, but is most importantly an abstract entity composed of all the brethren assembled. Opening the Lodge, then, must perforce embrace each and every one of those present.

Silence In The Lodge

In the Scottish Rite opening ritual, [2] the Master's opening words are 'Silence in Lodge'. The silence invoked is not only the absence of talk, but rather mental silence. The quieting down of the tumult of passions, fear, anger, brought by the brethren from the outside world, from their daily occupations and worries. Mental tranquility is required to focus the mind so it can fully participate in the Masonic work that is to take place.

The First Duty

The first duty of Masons assembled is to verify that they are under cover from the indiscretion of cowans. These, originally, were not strangers, but rather workers doing rough stone masonry without having been apprenticed. The meaning of the word then evolved to the present one, to designate those who have not been initiated into the Craft.

Some Masons believe that the Lodge is tyled by having the door closed, but the truth is you must have a brother (the 'Tyler') armed with a sword, standing outside the door. He 'covers' the Lodge, which explains his name in French and other languages (couvreur). Cover in this sense means to protect, to guard against danger (as insurance provides 'coverage'). Also, when brethren are asked to retire from the Lodge while it is open, are requested 'to cover the Lodge.'

We all know the legend, according to which the Tyler would stand peering through a displaced roof tile, looking for approaching strangers. Historically, however, the Tyler appears to have been the officer entrusted with drawing the 'Lodge', a symbolic sketch drawn on the floor, which eventually evolved into our present Trestleboard. At the conclusion of the ceremony, the Tyler would erase the drawing with mop and water. One well-known etching by Hogarth ('Night', reproduced in the Grand Lodge of Scotland Year Book for 1990, p. 83) shows the Tyler armed with his sword, and another figure holding the mop. Since the Tyler 'covers' the Lodge, the assembled brethren are 'under cover', which may mean either that they are working in secret, or that they are protected from interference from outside, or both.

Standing To Order

Standing to order comprises three elements: the position of the hands, the position of the feet, and the erect posture of the body. That is why no sign may be given while sitting or walking. It is an error to make something like a sign while sitting.

The order referred to by the sign has no relations to the soldier standing 'to order'. We are not waiting for orders, but rather ordering our thoughts. The position of our body must reflect the state of our mind. Disciplined thought is the prerequisite of any meaningful intellectual pursuit, Freemasonry included.

Order is, in fact, the distinctive mark of a Mason. In Lodge, we walk, speak, act, following a certain fixed pattern. Not by chance 'Ordo ab Chao' is a fundamental Masonic motto.

The Officers Of The Lodge

The ritual goes now into an extended dialogue between the Master and his officers, concerning their number, their situation in the Lodge and their duties.

The number seven is vastly significant in symbolism. It is the number of planets known in antiquity, the days of the week, the metals, etc.

The seven planets corresponded, in ancient lore, to seven spheres or 'heavens' circling around the earth. The idea of seven circles was used by Dante in the Divine Comedy, both for the heavens and for the circles of hell, which are their mirror image.

The order of the universe is best exemplified by the invariable movement of the celestial bodies, each in its own orbit, and each associated with a certain god having his or her own characteristics.

In the Lodge, the idea of order, of an immutable disposition connected with the sacramental space that is the Lodge, is expressed by the fixed places and duties of each officer within the Lodge. The seven officers mentioned in the Opening Ritual sit in their invariable places around the room, as so many planets within the consecrated space. Here, again, the ritual stressed the idea of order as central in Masonic philosophy. Only after the Lodge has been 'ordered' can work start. The Hebrew ritual, used in Israel, makes this unmistakable, for the Chaplain's prayer immediately preceding the actual opening sentence, begins with the words "as we merited to start our work in order . . ."

Light From The East

As part of the dialogue mentioned before, the Worshipful Master is likened to the rising sun in the east. The idea of light coming from the east is very old, dating from the earliest glimmerings of human existence. Men saw the sun rising every day from the east, bringing light, heat, life. The east was the most important cardinal point in old times (the north became important only after the invention of the magnetic compass). Old maps often place the east at the top.

Most primitive places of worship, like the stone circles spread all over Europe (Stonehenge, etc.), were oriented toward the east. This is really a redundancy, for 'oriented' itself means facing the east.

In Hebrew, an ancient language, the word for 'east' (kedem)

is also used to express the idea of forward movement, advancing (lehitkadem). Kedem also carries the meaning of antiquity, origin. Curiously, in Japanese, an equally ancient tongue, the ideogram for 'east' is also related to the ideogram for 'origin' or 'source'.

Order, then is related to the orient. When somebody has lost his direction, he is disoriented, he has lost his orient, his east.

In some Masonic rites, three candles are lit when opening the Lodge, and the first candle to be lit is always closest to the east.

The Mystic Vault

While the Volume of the Sacred Law and the tools are being arranged, three officers stand around the altar crossing their staffs, thus forming a sort of triangular pyramid. This is symbolically a mystic vault, connected with the traditions of the secret underground vault beneath King Solomon's Temple.

Why is the vault formed when opening the Lodge, and in all intermediate changes of degrees, but not for the closing ceremony? Because the vault indicates that we are entering the secret space where the Lodge meets, and we remain there as long as the Lodge is working. When closing the Lodge, we leave the secret place, and so we no longer build the symbolic vault.

The Trestleboard

Turning or uncovering the Trestleboard is the last piece of 'business' before the Lodge sets down to dispose of the order of the day.

The Trestleboard, which as also known as 'the Lodge', has a long and interesting history, which can be profitably studies by every brother. For our present purpose, suffice it to say that it represents in a condensed manner the entire symbolism of the Degree. Looking at the board in the course of the evening should remind every brother of the principal purpose of Masonic work: to ascend Jacob's Ladder, placed at the center of the First Degree Trestleboard, a representation of man's eternal aspiration for truth and spiritual elevation.

Chapter Notes

1 Searching for the God Within, Newsweek, 5 February 2001, p. 54.
2 The Scottish Rite ritual is used in many Lodges throughout the world. Almost all Latin-American Grand Lodges instruct or allow their Lodges to work in the Scottish Rite rituals.

Chapter 9

CAMPANELLA'S *CITY OF THE SUN*

Thomas Campanella was born in Stilo, a village in Calabria, Italy, in the year 1568. At a tender age (13 or 14 years), he entered the Dominican Order, where he remained for the rest of his days. He was a great admirer of Saint Thomas Aquinas, in whose honor he assumed his name, as his christening name was Giovanni Domenico. Nevertheless, throughout his life he fought against the theories of Aristotle and the Scholastics, of whom Saint Thomas is the exemplary representative.

Campanella was a prolific author, who started writing at the age of nineteen. Very soon after he came into conflict with the ecclesiastic authorities, because of his eager and curious mentality, and his admiration for the sciences that he, Campanella, believed to be called to conciliate with Christian, or rather Catholic, doctrine.

In his writings, Campanella insists again and again that we can arrive at an understanding of reality and of nature exclusively through our senses. This was totally opposed to the Aristotelian and scholastic method, founded on blind faith and pedantic abstraction divorced from any experimental verification.

Already in 1592 he was condemned, in an ecclesiastical trial in Naples, to return to his native Calabria, as punishment for having left the monastery. Among the accusations against him, we should note that he was charged with having sought the company of a rabbi called Abraham, magician and astrologer, who allegedly had introduced him to occultism. Furthermore, and this was a serious charge at the time, he was accused of having taken out books from the library without receiving permission.

The young friar was driven by thirst for knowledge. His intellectual appetite knew no boundaries. As he himself declared, he had studied the philosophies of Pythagoras, Epicurus, Plato, Thales, the Stoics and the Peripatetics [Aristotelians], of all ancient and modern sects, the laws of ancient peoples and of Hebrews, Turks, Persians, Moors, Chinese, Brahmins, Peruvians, Mexicans, Abysinians and Tartars. This was no empty boasting, because in his writings Campanella introduces numerous details and demonstrates his knowledge of the most diverse subjects.

Campanella was convinced that the world was approaching a millenary crisis, a total revolution in the order of things, that would create a fundamental change in the Church, at a time that this was conducting a furious battle against the Reform. This revolution, forecast by Campanella, would find expression in the most astounding progress of philosophy, science and politics. In certain respects, he can be regarded as a forerunner of the Rosicrucian manifestos.

In his opinion, philosophy is founded on facts and not words, it should discard opinions and turn to testimonies, that is to say, philosophy should give knowledge the first place, incorporating all the new discoveries. We should keep in mind that 'philosophy' at the time was a wide-ranging concept, including many areas of knowledge that today we designate as sciences.

Let us examine now some of the arguments raised by Campanella against abstract speculation. Saint Augustine, speculating, rejects the existence of the antipodes, while navigators have demonstrated it. Aristotle, speculating, maintains the incorruptibility, that is to say, immutability of the stars, while Galileo's telescope has discovered the phases of Venus. Zeno denies the existence of movement, while our senses, on the contrary, prove it irrefutably. Luther, speculating, rejects human freedom, on the pretext of divine predestination, 'but this writing pen I am holding, who can claim that I don't have the power to move it or not, to write or not write?'

Campanella's modernist and renovating spirit can be summarized in his observation, made in The City of the Sun, that 'this century of ours has more history in a hundred years that the world has had in four thousand, and in these hundred years more books have been written than in five thousand.'

The writer is deeply impressed by the recent discoveries and sees in them signs of the approaching millennium; the discovery of the new world, the compass, the printing press, the harquebus, receive philosophical explanations.

In 1600, as we know, another Italian thinker, Giordano Bruno, was burned at the stake as a heretic. Campanella did not suffer the same fate, but he was persecuted for his views and remained in prison, subject to privation and tortures, during 27 years.

His last years he spent in a monastery of his order in France, where he passed away on 21 May 1639.

The City of the Sun was written in Italian in 1602, while he was held in prison. He probably started writing while recovering from the torments of the inquisitors. The work appeared in a Latin translation in Frankfurt, in the year 1623. The second edition, still in Latin, came out in Paris in 1637. The first edition in the Italian original dates only from 1904, but the text is faulty. The best edition is that of Bobbio, of 1941, in both Italian and Latin.

In his book, Campanella describes an ideal society, in a state close to nature. The novel is written in the form of a dialogue between a seaman called Colon's pilot, and somebody called the Hospitaler, that is, a brother of the military order of Hospitalers of Saint John of Jerusalem. We know that Masonic Lodges are intimately connected with Jerusalem, the Hospitalers and particularly with Saint John. Symbolic Lodges are dedicated to Saint John and the feast days of the two Saint Johns (the Baptist and the Evangelist) are celebrated up to the present in many Masonic Lodges.[1]

The city of the sun is located on the island of Ceylon. 'The city is distributed into seven concentric circles, named after the seven planets.[2]

You enter from one to another through four roads and four gates facing the four quarters of the world.' Here we have a representation of the Masonic Lodge, with its four walls oriented to the four cardinal points. The number seven has important esoteric and symbolic meaning. The number and position of the Officers in the Lodge are related to the seven planets. The image of 'seven circles' had been used by Dante in his Divine Comedy (1314), where he describes both hell and heaven composed of seven circular stages.

In the center of the city is built a perfectly round temple, in whose center stands an altar. Here, again, we find the parallelism with the Masonic Lodge, and the difference of the altar's placement with that in a church.

'On the altar there is only a very large map of the world, painted with all the heavens, and another showing the earth.' In many Lodges, a terrestrial globe is placed on top of the B column, and a celestial globe or an armillary sphere on top of the J column.

'Seven lamps are always burning, named for the seven planets.' On the ceiling of the Lodge, usually seven stars are depicted. The resemblance of stars and lamps is evident.

The city, writes Campanella, is governed by a prince called Sun or the Metaphysic, assisted by three collateral princes named Pon, Sin and Mor, that is to say, Power, Wisdom and Love.

The parallelism with the government of a Masonic Lodge is astonishing. In effect, the three 'lights' of the Masonic Lodge are the Master and the two Wardens, who represent Wisdom, Strength and Beauty, respectively. Wisdom is identical in both cases. Power is Strength, and Love is Beauty, because when the author describes the functions of the Love 'prince', he enumerates the arts and crafts, and strangely enough, eugenics.

Power, knowledge and desire, or potency, wisdom and love, are the three 'primaries' that constitute, in Campanella's words, the 'essentiality' of a thing. Although they are separate, in fact they are the same and identical with the essence.

A similar idea is expressed when speaking of the 'three lights' of the Lodge, or the three who rule the Lodge. In the Royal Arch, this identification of three governing the Lodge (or the Chapter) is even clearer, and the Chapter cannot perform even its opening ritual without the concourse of the three principal officers. The Royal Arch, as we know, appeared simultaneously or soon after the creation of the premier Grand Lodge.

Of course, the solar triad may be conflated with all the traditional sacred triads, such as the Christian Trinity and so many others recorded in the history of religions.

An interesting fact is that the governor of the city is called Sol, the sun. The three principal officers of the Masonic Lodge represent, by their situation, the positions of the sun from dawn to dusk. In many rituals, also, movements on the floor of the Lodge are dextrorsum, or clockwise, resembling the apparent course of the sun on the sky of the northern hemisphere.

Let us continue with the description of the city and its inhabitants. 'All the young people are called brothers . . . and then, officers are attentive to everything in order to prevent any person from harming another within the fraternity.' Here Campanella gives the city its proper name.

All inhabitants' work. Campanella writes: 'Each wishing to be first in his work . . . whoever learns more arts and excels in them is regarded as nobler.'

The importance Masonry assigns to work is well known. Masonic meetings in many languages are known as 'works' (traveaux, trabajos). This concept of work is totally at variance with the contempt in which manual work was held in medieval Europe. 'Solarians [inhabitants of the city] make ridicule of us, who call craftsmen dishonorable, while we say that plebeians are those who don't learn any art and remain idle.'

There are still other parallelisms between Campanella's ideas and the traditions and symbols of our craft. The Solarians 'all dress in white during the day and red at night or out of the village.' 'Pride is considered a grave sin and they condemn an act of pride in the same manner as it has been committed. Therefore, nobody considers degrading to serve at the table, in the kitchen, or elsewhere, but they call it learning . . . and they don't have slaves.'

'If strangers want to become citizens, they may remain a month in the villages and one year in the city, and then they decide whether to accept them, with certain ceremonies and oaths.'

The Metaphysic, that is, the sun, 'presides as architect over all the sciences.' Campanella is not the first to assign the character of an architect to the supreme maker of the world, but his identification of architecture with the sun is remarkable.

In the temple, there are twenty-four priests. The temple, as mentioned before, is in the center of the city. The priests chant some psalms praising the Lord in the morning, night and midnight. Note this relation with the 24-inch ruler, and with the working hours of symbolic Lodges in the Scottish Rite.

'Prayers are directed toward the four cardinal points and, in the morning, toward the Orient, second, toward the occident, third toward the south, and fourth to the north.' If we take the first three movements, these are parallel to the movements of a brother who enters the Lodge, in the Scottish Rite, when saluting the three main officers of the Lodge.

'All their feasts are four main ones, which is to say, when the sun enters Aries, Cancer, Libra and Capricorn.' That means they celebrated solstices and equinoxes. Masons, too, celebrate the solstices.

A point that deserves underlining in Campanella's thoughts is his trust in reason. As Estebanez, one of his translators, points out, for Campanella, to live in accordance with reason has not only the same religious and moral meaning than Christianity, but is even sufficient to be saved. We must not assume that Campanella was against religion. Far from it, he is deeply religious and theist. For him the soul, for instance, is part of Eternal Reason in God, only one manifestation of the divinity. Religion is for him a congenital dimension of man and even, in a lower degree, of animals. Here, attention must be paid that the natural religion propounded by Campanella has the same content for all men who search for it through correct philosophy. This content is expressed in various rites and ceremonies, adapted to each society. This development, different for the diverse cultures, is called the added (addita) religion. Rites are accidental and may differ from one religion to another, without doubting their truthfulness. This concept of religion is perfectly in accord with that of Speculative Freemasonry.

'The Solarians hold as certain the immortality of the soul. They make of being, who is God, and nothingness, that is absence of being, the metaphysical principles of things.'

The duality of nature finds expression in pain and pleasure, the two spurs that direct everything. This reminds us of the sweet and bitter cup tasted by the initiate in the Scottish Rite ceremony, and also points to the symbolism of the checkerboard pavement.

Campanella mentions the appearance of a new star in Cassiopeia, 'that announces a great new monarchy and the reformation of the laws and the arts and prophets and renovation.'

This same theme appears in the first Rosicrucian manifesto of 1614, the Fama Fraternitatis, where new stars in Serpentarius and Cygnus are mentioned, with the same millenarian hope of renewal and reformation of the world.

The City of the Sun has other points of contact with the Rose-Croix. For instance, the Solarians, like the Rose-Croix brethren, speak all languages. Furthermore, the author of the Alchemical Wedding of Christian Rosenkreutz,3 Johan Valentin Andraea, is also the author of a work that is almost a copy of the City of the Sun. This is the Description of the Republic of Christianopolis, published in Strasbourg in 1619, that is, before Campanella's book. There can be little doubt that Andraea had access to a manuscript of the Italian's book, and this indicates the close relations existing among diverse European intellectuals of the time, all of them driven by a common ideal of reformation and universal fraternity.

Frances Yates, the English historian, believes that Campanella was aware of the hermetic and cabalistic traditions. We cannot exclude the possibility that alchemists and cabalists of the 16th and 17th centuries were connected by a secret brotherhood, whose organization may have been informal, but allowing them to maintain contact and exchange ideas and discoveries, sometimes running against prevailing religious dogma. Such a development may be discerned in the Rosicrucian manifestos.

To conclude, let us place Campanella within the history of ideas. Campanella is numbered among the Renaissance thinkers who came under the influence of the Jewish Kabalah and adapted it to Christian doctrines. This Christian Cabala, exemplified by Pico della Mirandola and Francesco Giorgi, also incorporated elements of hermetic philosophy (that is, based on the writing attributed to Hermes Trismegistus), magic and alchemy. This philosophy received new impulse under the form of the Rose-Croix at the beginning of the 17th century. The Rosicrucians disappeared in the European continent, but some refugees found asylum in England, where the Rosicrucian manifestos were translated into English at the time of Cromwell (1599-1658). Later, a violent reaction broke out against the Hermetic-Cabalist magic and then, in my opinion, a movement was produced for the integration of Rosicrucians and magicians-cabalists into the Lodges of operative masons, who had started to accept non-operative members. The hermetic philosophers found in Masonic Lodges the protection of secret and silence that enabled them to continue their research.

Bibliography

Campanella, Thomas, La citdu soleil, Spanish translation and commentary by Emilio G. Estebanez, Zero, Madrid 1984.
Yates, Frances, Giordano Bruno and the Hermetic Tradition, Routledge and Kegan Paul, London 1964.
Yates, Frances, The Occult Philosophy in the Elizabethan Age, Ark Paperbacks, London 1983.

Chapter Notes

1 They are often called "Solsticial Feasts", because they fall on or close to the solstices.
2 That is to say, those known in antiquity as the planets: sun, moon, Mercury, Venus, Mars, Jupiter and Saturn
3 Widely regarded as the third Rosicrucian publication.

Chapter 10

AN ESOTERIC VIEW OF THE ROSE-CROIX DEGREE

The principal task of the Freemason, which is to improve his own character, eliminating those negative traits that might exist in his personality and developing his moral and spiritual resources (what is known as "polishing the raw stone") is in great measure the result of the interaction among brethren within and without the Lodge. However, the most important means to advance in this work is necessarily introspection and meditation, that is, reflection and self-awareness.

Gnothi Seauton

"Know thyself" is a symbolic aspect of Freemasonry that in the Scottish Rite Initiation ceremony (in the First Degree) is announced already in the candidate's first contact with our Order, in the Chamber of Reflection, where he finds inscriptions such as Know Thyself and, most important, V.I.T.R.I.O.L. (which in Latin means: "Visit the interior of the earth and rectifying will find the hidden stone"). The stone that the neophyte is invited to find is, without doubt, his own pure soul.

Purifying his spirit (rectifying as in rectified alcohol, or correcting by removing errors), the Mason will find the symbolic stone, that is, the moral perfection he seeks.

Although these and other intimations are introduced in the first three degrees of Freemasonry, they are tangential to the introspective nature of Masonic work, especially evident in the Hiramic legend, but without exploring more deeply the esoteric aspects of inner development. It is only when the Mason reaches the 18th degree of the Scottish Rite, the mystical degree par excellence, that he faces inescapably the mystic experience and is induced to apply this experience to his own spiritual development.

Preparatory Stages

The preceding degrees, until the 14th inclusive, deal with various aspects of the Hiramic legend, examining themes such as duty, faithfulness, the knowledge and virtues that characterize a Mason.

A leitmotiv throughout these degrees is the lost word, which is finally recovered at some point during the 18th degree.

The first two of the "Chapter" degrees, which serve as a transition between the Lodge of Perfection and the Rose-Croix Chapter, deal with the Second Temple of Jerusalem, built by the Jews returning from the Babylonian captivity, and who brought with them a rich cultural baggage (including the names of the months in Hebrew) and also certain features of oriental mysticism, such as the belief in the afterlife, which did not exist earlier in Hebrew traditions.

The third capitular degree that of Knights of the East and the West, marks a turning point in its content, no longer referring to the destruction of the Jerusalem Temple, ravaged by the Roman legions, but to the celestial Jerusalem, linking heaven and earth

As Naudon remarks in his commentary on the higher degrees, there can be little doubt that this degree was designed to create a preamble to the Rose-Croix degree and was introduced after it.

The 17th degree has some interesting characteristics, such as the use of black gloves, as in the "elu" or "vengeance" degrees. Black, as we know, represents the nigredo, the first stage of the alchemical work.

Allegory Versus Literal Meaning

Let us now examine the 18th degree itself. It is not my intention to describe the ritual or the "secrets" of this degree. All this has been frequently published and the interested reader can easily find this information in one of the books in the bibliography at the end of this paper. What we would like to do is to show that the Christian aspects of the ceremony - and there are many - can and must be understood in their symbolic meaning, as esoteric language.

Any literal interpretation would lead to absurd conclusions. To give an example, a literal interpretation of the Third-degree legend would produce the grotesque image of a rotten corpse somehow rising from its grave and becoming incarnate in the candidate.

Furthermore, at least for this writer, a literal interpretation of the 18th degree ritual would be close to sacrilege. A simulacrum of one of the key events in Holy Scripture would be in danger of becoming a parody.

Only if we understand the ritual as allegorical can we avoid this danger.

In truth, all Masonic rituals are based on allegory which, according to one dictionary is a fiction that presents an object to the mind, so as to evoke the thought of another object (Larousse). Notice the word fiction.

Albert Pike, the great reformer of Scottish Rite rituals, refers to this problem in his explanations to the candidate before the ceremony of elevation to the 18th degree: 'All the emblems, forms and ceremonies of Masonry are symbolical of great primitive truths, which each one is at liberty to interpret in accordance with his own faith' (Magnum Opus, XVIII.5).

Taking into account, these considerations, the study of the 18th degree, or any other Masonic degree, must start from the premise that we must approach the text as allegory, as representing something else.

This is not the place to enter into a discussion on the fine distinction between allegory and symbol. The two are intimately related but, as clearly demonstrated by Alleau, allegory is a rhetorical process, related to language and interpretation, i.e., reason, while the symbol leads directly from the significant and the signification to the Signifier.

According to the exegete Origenes, sacred texts must be studied on three levels: the literal texts, the soul of the text and the spirit of the text (Alleau, p. 120). Not by chance the cover of his book is illustrated by a seven-petal rose, taken from the Summum Bonum of Robert Fludd, a defense of the Rosicrucian fraternity.

A similar attitude must be adopted when analyzing Masonic rituals. They must be studied on three levels: literal, symbolic and esoteric.

The Christian Explanation

The school of thought that maintains that the Rose-Croix ritual must be understood as a Masonic version of the Passion of Christ finds support in the many obvious parallels between elements of the ceremony and passages of the Gospels, such as the darkness enveloping the earth, the number 33, the mystical supper, and others that it is unnecessary to detail.

Then, we must consider the three theological virtues: Faith, Hope and Charity (which also appear on the Tracing Board of the First Degree), the extinction of the lights and other particulars.

Some reflection, however, will make it clear that each of these points in the 18th decree ceremony admits other explanations, of a symbolic and esoteric nature.

The broken tools, for instance, and the darkness of the chamber in the first part of the ceremony, do they not represent the confusion and impotence of man, wandering through a world full of evil, insecure about his way, looking for an exit to light? Is this not a frequent human experience? Is this not a lesson that the candidate should learn, that appealing to his own inner spiritual resources, it is possible to move from darkness to light?

Tearing one's clothes is a well-known signal of bereavement. To this day, Jews make a symbolic tear of their garment as part of the burial ceremony for a relative. The renting of the Temple's veil is akin to this category of ideas. It is not necessarily identified with the crucifixion, but it represents the sorrow that every man should feel when witnessing the triumph of the forces of evil.

Another impressive image is the cubic stone distilling blood and water. This is an alchemical symbol. The red blood and the white water are two alchemical elements, representing sulfur and mercury, respectively. This appears explicitly in an illustration of an alchemical manuscript of the 18th century (reproduced on plate 18 of the book Alchemy by Klossowsky de Rola). The knight, in that illustration, wields a sword and is dressed in the alchemical colors. He holds a shield with a motto meaning "make one water from two, etc."

Bayard (pp. 103-120) has made a detailed analysis of each of the elements of the ritual of our degree, explaining its historical development and it's allegorical and spiritual meanings. The reader can refer to Bayard's book, since within the framework of this paper we cannot examine too many of the symbols involved.

The Acronym INRI

Let us examine now one of the most conspicuous symbols of the Rosicrucian degree, the four letters I.N.R.I.

First, a remarkable parallel links this acronym with the ineffable name of the Deity in the Bible, the Tetragammaton. Both are composed of four letters, one of which is repeated. In Hebrew, the letters are Yod-Heh-Vav-Heh.

Of course, the first reaction of a reader with an elementary acquaintance with the Bible is to give a Christian interpretation to the acronym: Iesus Nazarenus Rex Iudeorum, the inscription on the cross.

However, an examination of various rituals of the 18th degree in different places and times, reveals a wide range of Masonic interpretations, such as:

Igne Natura Renovatur Integra
(Nature is completely renewed by fire)

Ignis Natura Renovat Integram
(Fire completely renews nature)

Ignem Natura Regenerando Integrat
(By regeneration, nature maintains the integrity of fire)

In Nobilis Regnat Iehovah (or Iesus)
(Jehovah (or Jesus) reigns among noble men)

Iesus Nascente Ram Innovatur
(Ascending Jesus renews the branch)

Igne Nitrum Roris Invenitor
(Dew meets niter and fire)

Insignia Naturae Ratio Illustrat
(Reason illuminates the nature's symbols)

Inter Nos Regnat Indulgentia
(Among us reigns goodness)

Intra Nobis Regnum Iehova
(The Kingdom of God is within us)

Iustum Necare Reges Impios
(It is just to kill impious kings)

Iustitia Nunc Reget Imperia
(Justice now rules empires)

In Neci Renascor Integer
(In death one is reborn intact and pure)

    Another explanation mentioned by Naudon claims that the four letters are the initials of Judea, Nazareth, Raphael and Judah. In Hebrew, Judea and Judah are written with an initial "I".
    Still another explanation is given by Albert Pike in his Magnum Opus: the four letters are initials of the words Infinity, Nature, Reason and Immortality.
    As if all this were not sufficient, the acronym has also been attributed to four Hebrew words: Iam, Nur, Ruakh and Ieveshah, which represent the four elements: water, fire, air and earth. This requires some latitude in the interpretations, because I am actually means sea, and only by synecdoche can it be taken to represent water.

The existence of so many and diverse explanations, formulated by different Masonic writers in the course of time, demonstrates that the literal or Biblical explanation is certainly insufficient and probably erroneous within the Masonic context.

The Cross And The Rose

We should examine, even superficially, the central symbolism of the degree: the cross and the rose. Sometimes, the cross is represented with four roses at the extremities of the two posts, but more often the cross is at the center, at the intersection of the vertical and horizontal lines.

The cross, as been frequently noted, did not become a Christian symbol until the 6th century. It has a long history before that, in many civilizations, from India to Egypt. Among the ancient Egyptians, the cross crowned by a ring, the ankh, represented both life and death. Sahir Erman remarks that the horizontal line of the cross also represents death, while the vertical one symbolizes life.

Its main symbolism appears to be the conjunction of two worlds, human and celestial. In general, the cross represents the integration of opposites, vertical and horizontal, spiritual and material, feminine and masculine, yin and yang.

Jose Catellani mentions that in the Indian city of Benares, in the ruins of an old temple can be found a cross with mystic rose in the center, inscribed within an equilateral triangle. This, as Castellani himself underlines, does not prove the existence of Masons or Rosicrucians thousands of years ago, but rather than the symbolic use of these images dates from ancient times. The cross, like the triangle and the circle, is one of the primary symbols of our consciousness. No complete explanation of their meaning can be given, because they are embedded in the deepest levels of our mind.

The rose, on its part, is a symbol of perfection and mystery. Erman points out that the rose is also a symbol of love, Amor in

Latin, which can also be interpreted as "A-Mor," that is, the negation of death. The rose embracing the cross thus represents immortality, and the way to achieve it, which is love.

The rose is also an important alchemical symbol. The number of petals is meaningful as well as their color, which may be red, white or black, the three principal alchemical colors.

The Rose-Croix

As mentioned above, Albert Pike stated clearly the principles of Freemasonry as a universal philosophy, allowing the faithful of various religions to sit together and work in harmony for the progress of Humanity as a whole.

Pike summarized the teachings of this degree in these words: "The unity, immutability and goodness of God; the immortality of the Soul; and the ultimate defeat and extinction of evil and wrong and sorrow, by a Redeemer or Messiah, yet to come, if he has not already appeared . . . It replaces the three pillars of the old Temple, with three that have been already explained to you - Faith [in God, mankind and man's self]; Hope [in the victory over evil, the advancement of Humanity, and in a hereafter] and Charity [relieving the wants, and tolerant of the errors and faults of others]. To be trustful, to be hopeful, to be indulgent; these, in an age of selfishness, of ill opinion of human nature, of harsh and bitter judgment, are the most important Masonic Virtues, and the true supports of every Masonic Temple. And they are the old pillars of the Temple under different names. For he only is wise who judges others charitably; he only is strong who is hopeful; and there is no beauty like a firm faith in God, our fellows and ourselves" (XVIII.19).

This is a moving and correct statement of the fundamental tenets of Freemasonry, not only the 18th degree. The "old pillars" to which Pike refers are Strength, Beauty and Wisdom (or Love), which in the Lodge are represented by the three principal officers. Pike carefully chooses his words so as to make them acceptable to believers of all faiths.

And yet, Pike's statement does not go far enough. It does not explain the question, why wrap these principles in the alchemical clothing of the Rosicrucians. What is the relation between Freemasonry and the Rose-Croix Fraternity?

The first mention we have, connecting Freemasonry with Rosicrucianism dates from 1638, only 24 years after the publication of the first Rosicrucian manifesto, the Fama Fraternitatis in 1614. This mention appears in Henry Adamson's Muses Threnodie, an account in verse of Perth, published in Edinburgh, and it also contains the first written reference to the Mason Word:

For what we do presage is not in grosse,
For we be brethren of the Rosie Crosse;
We have the Mason word and second sight,
Things for to come we can foretell aright.

The fact that a connection is made between Freemasonry and Rose-Croix at such an early stage is most significant. Furthermore, a 'divertisement' published in Poor Robin's Intelligence for 10 October 1676, mentions both "the Ancient Brother-hood of the Rosy-Cross" and the "Company of accepted Masons" as dining together.

More important still, in a letter of 'A.Z.' printed in the Daily Journal of 5 September 1730, the writer states:

there is a Society abroad, from whom the English Free Masons . . . have copied a few Ceremonies, and take great Pains to persuade the World that they are derived from them, and are the same with them. They are called Rosicrucians . . . On this Society has our Moderns, as we have said, endeavored to ingraft themselves, tho' they know nothing of their more material Constitutions, and are acquainted only with some of their Signs of Probation and Entrance . . . (Knoop, Jones and Hamer, p. 27).

Although Knoop, Jones & Hamer dispute the suggestion that the English Freemasons would attempt to trace their origins from the Rosicrucians, these references prove that from its very beginnings, Freemasonry included a spiritual and esoteric component, very different from its labor or operative aspects.

It is beyond the scope of this paper to examine the history, ideology and symbolism of the Rosicrucian Fraternity. Numerous, better qualified researchers, have already done so. We recommend particularly the books of McIntosh and Yates (see the Bibliography at the end).

What is interesting is the question, why our brethren of the 18th century included this degree in the Scottish Rite system (and before that, in its antecedent Rites).

Perhaps the best explanation is that proposed by Colin Wilson in his preface to the book on Rosicrucians by Christopher McIntosh:

"This [human desire to turn inward to a world of truth that he feels resides in his own depths], I believe, explains why Rosicrucianism has continued to exert its grip on the Western mind. It is not because we are hopelessly gullible, or because we would like to believe in absurd fantasies. In a legend like that of Christian Rosenkreuz, we seem to catch a glimpse of what we ought to be, and what we could be."

The same Christopher, explaining to Wilson how he came to write his book, relates that "When I began . . . I intended to examine Rosicrucianism simply as a rather curious historical phenomenon without really expecting to find that it contained a teaching of any real depth or coherence. Since then not only has my attitude changed - I have become much more pro-occult - but also found during my researches that Rosicrucianism goes deeper than I had realized, and does contain something valuable and coherent. So you could say that this book has been an important experience in my life. It has taught me that sooner or later anyone studying these subjects from an academic point of view has to make the decision whether they are going to take a personal stance for or against."

In other words, the rich symbolic contents of this degree, the manner in which it penetrates to the roots of our spiritual being, bestows a unique opportunity to the Mason, making him face questions that he generally ignores in daily life. The problems of his own nature, of the possible transformation that he himself must undergo, the transmutation from coarse matter to luminous essence.

Inner Transformation

In the 18th degree, the Mason faces a potent symbolism. If he has received a Christian education, he will be moved by the emotional impact of the apparent parallelism between the Masonic ceremony and his religious beliefs. Even if his religious background is different, he cannot remain apathetic to the sharp contrasts between the various parts of the ceremony, the transition from darkness to light, from sorrow to hope to joy; from the deepest despond to the merry conviviality of the shared repast.

The message conveyed by the symbolism of this degree has multiple levels and constitutes a challenge to the candidate's imagination. It stirs him and drives him to explore the inner processes illustrated by the circumstances described in the liturgy of the degree. Revealing in this connection is the commentary of McIntosh, searching for an explanation of the fact that the first edition of the Fama Fraternitatis included in the same volume another work entitled Allgemeine und General Reformation der gantzen weiten Welt (The Universal and General Reformation of the Whole Wide World) - an extract from the Italian author Trajano Boccalini's allegorical satire, Ragguali di Parnasso (News from Parnassus), McIntosh writes:

Andreae may have reasoned that by issuing the Fama with the General Reformation he could make the point that an inner reformation within men's minds and hearts must precede any external reformation and that the account given in the Fama had to be seen in this light (p.49).

In other words, from their beginning, the author or authors of the Rosicrucian manifestos made clear that the first step for the reformation of the world must necessarily be the reformation of the spirit, and this is precisely the premise of the 18th degree of Freemasonry, properly understood.

This invitation to introspection and meditation appears specifically prescribed in some rituals of the 18th degree used even today (e.g., in Mexico and Spain).

Even if the ritual book for the ceremony does not explicitly call for a period of meditation, serious reflection on the esoterism of the degree will lead the Knight Rose-Croix to the road of spiritual exercise, inciting him to concentrate his thoughts and his will in order to discover and make conscious the light burning within himself, identifying with it until achieving the mystic experience.

Conclusion

The Scottish Rite, by offering the Rose-Croix degree to its members, is only opening a door. Not everybody will profit from the opportunity to go through it and delve into this field of study. What matters is that the opportunity exists. This, after all, is the Masonic method and the philosophy of our Orden in all its structures: we put the tools in the hands of the brother and let him labor according to his capacity and development. Without compulsion, without prize, except for the progress to a further degree, which will present new challenges.

To restrict the explanation of the 18th degree to a paraphrase of the Passion of Jesus is not only simplistic, and perhaps irreverent, but ignores the complex symbolism contained in the degree and the purpose of its inclusion in the ladder of spiritual ascent configured by the degrees of the Scottish Rite. A better understanding of its esoteric dimensions will enrich the brother as an individual and the Order as a whole.

Bibliography

Alleau, Rene: La science des symboles, Payot, 1976.
Bayard, Jean Pierre: Le symbolisme mañonique des Hauts Grades, Editions Du Prisme, Paris 1975.
Bonvicini, Eugenio: La Storia dei Rosa+Croce e della loro Incidenza sulla Massoneria.
Castellani, Jose: A Orden Rosacruz e a Maconaria, A Maconaria no Estado de Sao Paulo.
Cirlot, J.L., Dictionary of Symbols, Dorset Press, NY 1991.
Erman, Sahir: Comentaires des Hauts Grades du R E A A , Supreme Council for Turkey, Istanbul 1990.
Gargia Pelayo y Gross, Ramon, Pequeno Larousse en color, Paris 1972.

Klein, Ernest: A Comprehensive Etymological Dictionary of the Hebrew Language for Readers of English, Carta, Jerusalem 1987.

Klossowski de Rola, Stanislas: Alchemy, Thames & Hudson, London 1973.

Knoop, Jones and Hamer: Early Masonic Pamphlets, QCCC, London 1978.

McIntosh, Christopher: The Rosicrucians, Crucible, UK 1980 (1987).

Naudon, Paul: Histoire, Rituels et Tuilleur des Hauts Grades Maconiques, Dervy- Livres, Paris 1984.

Peterson, Norman D.: "Mottos & Foreign Quotations in the Scottish Rite", The Plumbline, Vol. 3, No.2, June 1994.

Pike, Albert: The Magnum Opus or Great Work, 1857 (reprint by Kessinger, Kila, MT, USA 1992).

Yates, Frances, A., The Rosicrucian Enlightenment, Paladin, 1975.

Chapter 11

THE DEAD SEA SCROLLS

During centuries, the only known references about the Essenes were a few brief mentions in the writings of Plinius, Philo and Flavius Josephus. Only in April 1947 this situation changed, when an Arab shepherd, looking for a stray goat, found several large ceramic jars hidden in a cavern, up the hill near the northern shore of the Dead Sea. The jars contained some rolls of parchment wrapped in cloth. These are the famous Dead Sea scrolls, which since their discovery and decipherment have caused a profound revolution in the thinking about the history of the Jewish religion in the crucial period of early first century of the C.E., and thrown new light on the origins of Christianity.

Later searches in other near-by caves resulted in the discovery of other rolls and numerous parchment fragments. The total number of scrolls, when they were intact, is estimated to have been over one thousand; until now, 870 different parchments have already been identified. The fragments differ in size, some of them are no larger than a thumbnail. In one cavern alone (N 4) some 15,000 fragments were found.

Although we refer to the Dead Sea manuscripts as parchment scrolls, some were written on papyrus, and one is written on a copper foil. They are written in several Semitic languages, although mostly in Hebrew.

An important point to remember is that until the discovery of these scrolls, scholars were of the opinion that in the beginning of the Christian era Hebrew was a dead language, used only by the educated few, such as Latin was in the Middle Ages of Europe. The Rabbinical Hebrew used in the literature of the years 200 and later was regarded as a scholastic invention, not a language of daily use. This belief led historians to conclude that the Gospels could not have been written originally in Hebrew or Aramaic.

The discovery of the scrolls refuted these opinions. It became clear that the Jews of the Second Temple period (after the return of the Babylonian exile) used simultaneously both Hebrew and Aramaic. These two languages are closely related. In writing, however, the ancient Hebrews preferred using the Biblical language, that is Hebrew.

The history of the discovery of these documents and their vicissitudes until finding suitable repository at the hands of archeologists could serve to write a novel. I shall try to summarize very briefly the main course of events.

As already mentioned, at the end of Spring of 1947, some Bedouin shepherds of the Taamire tribe discovered by chance the jars containing scrolls. One of the parchment bundles, later denominated the "Isaiah Manuscript", was offered for sale to an Arab antiquities merchant in the town of Bethlehem.

To understand what happened then we must remember that at the time Palestine was still under the rule of the British Army, while the United Nations discussed the fate of the British Mandate that was reaching its conclusion. There was still contact between the Arab and Jewish communities in Palestine, but venturing into certain sectors had become hazardous, and violent confrontations were becoming more frequent from day to day.

The Arab merchant did not assign much importance to the old parchment, believing it had no great value, and he refused to pay the sum asked by the Bedouin: twenty English pounds. The Bedouin then turned to a merchant belonging to the Syrian Orthodox community, living in Bethlehem, and this made contact with his friend, a Jerusalem merchant. In this roundabout way, the discovery of the scrolls came to the attention of

The Syrian Orthodox Metropolitan (equivalent to an archbishop) of the Saint Mark monastery, in the old city of Jerusalem. After a short while, the archbishop, Monsignor Atanasios Samuel, bought four of the scrolls. He then showed them to several persons, among them some members of the Biblical and Archeological College of the Dominicans, in Jerusalem, who also considered the manuscripts as being of recent origin, and having little value.

Around the month of August of 1948, Bishop Samuel informed a Jewish physician, Dr. Brown, about the discovery of the scrolls and asked his opinion, Dr. Brown communicated this information to Professor Yehuda Magnes, President of the Hebrew University of Jerusalem, who in turn transmitted the news to the University Library and asked that some manuscript experts examine the scrolls. Two envoys from the University Library visited the Syrian monastery and the bishop showed them some of the manuscripts, not revealing their source, but rather telling them that they had been found in one of the monasteries of his community near the Dead Sea. The library clerks, after examining the manuscripts, concluded they lacked the necessary expertise to determine their antiquity, and proposed a further examination by somebody better qualified for the task. However, before the Hebrew University could send its experts, Bishop Samuel decided to return to Syria, taking the scrolls with him.

That was during a turbulent period of armed struggle between Arab and Jewish groups, resulting in numerous casualties.

Let's go back in time. On 25 November 1947 a Jerusalem antiquary showed to Professor Eliezer Sukenik, of the Hebrew University, a parchment fragment written in the old "square" Hebrew alphabet, which Sukenik immediately identified as similar to the inscriptions on sarcophagi dating from the Hashmonean era, that is, the two centuries before and the first century following the birth of Jesus.

The antiquary related that he had obtained the fragment from a Bethlehem merchant, who had been offered some scrolls by Bedouins. The Bethlehem merchant then asked Professor Sukenik's opinion, whether it was worth to purchase those scrolls, and whether the professor would be interested in purchasing them in turn.

To make the story short, on 29 November Sukenik bought from the Bethlehem intermediary three parchment rolls, and also two of the ceramic jars that contained them. On that same day, the United Nations voted the end of the British Mandate and the partition of Palestine. Arab armies immediately invaded the country from all sides, and Israel's war of independence started. This caused the complete break of relations between the Arab and Jewish communities in Palestine. Nevertheless, Professor Sukenik succeeded in maintaining contact with the Arabs involved in the matter.

At that time, one of the workers in the University Library related to Professor Sukenik the episode with the Syrian archbishop, and Sukenik immediately realized that those parchments had the same origin. He tried to visit the Monastery of Saint Mark to examine the manuscripts, but the monastery was already cut off from the Jewish sector of Jerusalem and travel between the two sides was impossible. At the end of January 1948, Sukenik received a message from Anton Kiraz, a member of the Syrian community, who communicated that he had in his possession several old parchments and wanted to show them. Those were the scrolls of Bishop Samuel. Sukenik managed to find a neutral place to meet with Kiraz. After some negotiations, they finally met in the Y.M.C.A. building, close to the Old City but still within the Jewish sector. When Sukenik examined the scrolls brought by Kiraz, he realized they belonged to the same group of those he had already purchased. He took three of the scrolls to be examined by other experts, and they all concluded they were authentically old.

A protracted negotiation now started to purchase the scrolls. David Ben-Gurion, then President of the Jewish Agency, and later Israel's first Prime Minister, was approached and his approval was secured to destine the necessary funds, although the war made more urgent demands on the scant resources of the Jewish population. Meanwhile, however, the Syrian Orthodox decided to wait until the end of hostilities, to get a better price, and then, through the American College of Oriental Studies in Jerusalem, the manuscripts were transferred to the United States.

On 11 April of that same year (1948) a publication in the United States disclosed that the Americans scholars in Jerusalem had identified for the first time some of the Dead Sea manuscripts as belonging to a period preceding the destruction of the Jerusalem Temple, in the year 70 C.E.

These news evoked great interest in scientific circles. Sukenik then decided to publish a first study on the parchments, a booklet that appeared with the title "The Hidden Scrolls" (Hameguilot Hagnuzot).

To conclude this story, Professor Sukenik purchased three scrolls, while his son, the archeologist and army general Yigael Yadin, eventually bought in New York the four scrolls owned by he Syrian archbishop. An eighth scroll, the important Temple Parchment, was purchased by Yadin after the end of the Six Days War of 1967, when Jerusalem was finally reunited.

The seven original scrolls are now exhibited in the Museum of the Book, part of Jerusalem's Israel Museum. They are the following: Manual of Discipline, presently known as Character of a Sectarian Jewish Association, Histories of the Patriarchs, Psalms of Thanksgiving, A Commentary on Habbakuk, the War between the Sons of Light and the Sons of Darkness, and two copies of the book of Isaiah.

Apart from the scrolls, numerous parchment fragments have been discovered, whose translation and publication has taken many decades and caused sharp disputes in scholarly circles. They are kept at present in Jerusalem's Rockefeller Museum.

The antiquity of the Dead Sea scrolls was conclusively proven when some samples were tested in April 1991 in a Swiss laboratory, dating them around the beginning of the Christian era. Archeologists, basing themselves on the writing, had already reached the same conclusion, that the parchments could not be of a later date than the year 68, when Roman legions reached Qumran and the settlement there was liquidated.

What interests us in to take a look at the content of the scrolls, written two thousand years ago, and to advance some theories about their possible connection with Masonic legends and traditions.

Qumran

First, let as learn something about the people who wrote the scrolls, the circumstances when they were written, and this will help us to judge their significance.

Near the caverns where the scrolls were found are the ruins of Qumran, a structure that has been identified by archeologists as the first known monastery in the Western world. There is little doubt that the place was inhabited for a long period of time, lasting over a century. The first archeologist to make scientific excavations in the place, Father De Vaux, of the Biblical School of Jerusalem, arrived to the conclusion that this was a meeting place for the Essenes, and since the settlement is not very large, De Vaux assumed that most of the members of the sect lived in the nearby caves, and came down to the main building only to meet, shared the meals, take ritual baths and pray together.

In the course of years, this theory was disputed by other researchers, but the latest discoveries of archeologist Magen Broschi (who was for many years Curator of the Dead Sea Scrolls in the Israel Museum) and Dr. Hanan Eshel of Bar-Ilan University, confirmed irrefutably De Vaux's assumption. These archeologists discovered paths leading from the Qumran ruins to the caves, and found there 2000-year old sandal nails, as well as coins of the epoch and pottery.

The Essenes

Who were the inhabitants of Qumran, who wrote or preserved these parchment documents in the Dead Sea caverns?

The Essenes were one of the minor factions of the Jewish people in the Hashmonean period. The main groups, as we know, were the Pharisees and the Saducees.

After the conquest of the Middle East by Alexander the Great, and after his death in the year 323 B.C.E., Palestine became a battleground between two of his generals: Seleucus, who governed Syria, and Ptolomy in Egypt. A descendant of Seleucus, Antioch Epiphanes IV, tried to impose paganism on the Jews, introducing the cult of Zeus and the other Greek gods. This resulted in the revolt of the Maccabees in the year 165 B.C. After a cruel war, the Jews, under the leadership of Judah Maccabee (Maccabee in Hebrew means " The Hammer") defeated the Greek generals and achieved independence. Although Judah Maccabee died in battle, his descendants, beginning with John Hircanus, continued the Hashmonean dynasty, marked by continuous fraternal wars and the growing menace of Roman power.

It was in this tempestuous period of history that the Essenes separated themselves from the main current of Judaism, constituting what today would be called an ultra-orthodox sect. The considered that the end of the world was near (the apocalypses), and they tried to observe strictly all the prescriptions of the Torah, that is, the Pentateuch, the first five books of the Bible. Some writers indicate that Saint John the Baptist may have been a member of the sect, and even Jesus has been mentioned as a possible member.

The name Essene (issi in Hebrew) means pious. The Essenes were ascetic, practicing frequent fasts and daily ritual baths. They studied the holy writings assiduously and conducted themselves democratically.

The Essenian Organization

Among the Dead Sea scrolls there are two, in particular, that throw light on the organization and principles of the Essenes. This is the scroll called "Manual of Discipline" and the "Zadokite Document". The first is included among the Qumran scrolls, while a copy of the second was discovered at the end of the 19th century by Solomon Schechter in the Gnizah (storeroom) of the Ezra synagogue in Fostat, the old quarter of Cairo. It's a known fact that old Hebrew religious texts are not destroyed, because the name of God appears on them, but they are stored in a special repository or storeroom of the synagogue, the Gnizah.

The Community Rule

We shall now examine some of the rules of the Dead Sea community, and decide whether they bear some resemblance to Masonic traditions.

When a person desired to join the community, he had to undertake to respect God and men, practice virtue and avoid evil. This is quite similar to a passage in the opening ritual of the lodge in the First Degree of the Scottish Rite. When the question is asked, for what purpose are we assembled, the answer is 'to raise temples to Virtue and to dig dungeons to vice'. Also, in the initiation ritual, the candidate is enjoined to practice choose the path of virtue and not that of vice. The statement of belief in the Supreme Being is also a required part of the initiation ceremony.

The community examined the background of the candidate, his character, and his fulfillment of religious precepts. Each person was then inscribed in a particular rank, coming under the authority of a superior.

The candidate had to love the sons of the light. This is an important detail. Masons are also known as "Children of the Light". Receiving the light is the crucial point of the initiation ceremony. The sun, and its light, plays a prominent role in Masonic rituals.

When the candidate was initiated in the community, the priests pronounced a special blessing. The members of the community were divided into three classes: the priests (Cohanim), Levites and the people. This brings to mind the division between Apprentices, Fellow-Crafts and Master Masons.

Every year, the progress of every member of the community was assessed, from the oldest to the youngest initiate. Each one was classified anew, "so that no one may be reduced in his state or exalted above his appointed place".

Members of the community took meals together, prayed together and held debates. "In the presence of the priest, all take seats according to their respective ranks, and the same order is adopted to speak."

This is also the tradition in Lodge, where the Brethren take their seats according to their degree, and in the Scottish Rite lodges, they are also granted the right to speak following a set order determined by rank.

In the community's debates, all could take part, following their order, but no one could interrupt another, nor speak before his turn, according to his rank. Nobody could speak about matters other than those of interest to the entire community.

This reminds us of the procedure of Masonic debates, and the 'raisings', or 'General welfare' part in the ritual, when all the brethren are invited to speak up.

If a person wanted to join, he was interrogated by the Superintendent concerning his intelligence and his behavior. Then, if considered suitable, he was presented to the general assembly, where every one gave his opinion, and his admission or rejection was decided by vote. One of the rules concerning admission to the community specifies that "no person with a physical defect, crippled on both legs or arms, lame, blind, deaf, dumb, or having a visible physical defect, can join".

A similar restriction appears in the old Masonic documents.

If the candidate was accepted and took an obligation to comply with the rules of the community, he was admitted on trial for a year, during which time the initiate could take part in the discussions only as an Observer. After this first year, he was again examined to verify his progress. If they were considered adequate, he was allowed to continue for a second year, but then he had to bring his belongings and the tools of his trade, which were turned over to the "Minister of Work" for safekeeping. Only after the second year, following a further examination, he was formally accepted, sworn in and inscribed in the register of the Brethren of the Community.

This succession of trial periods and examinations is also reflected in the practices in our Lodges. The candidate is examined before initiation, and later, before advancing to each further degree.

The neophyte had to imitate the purity of his masters, that is, practice the rules of decency and walk in perfect sanctity. He undertook to follow a long road in search of enlightenment.

The congregation counted twelve brothers and three priests well versed in the Law, called "of perfect sanctity". This brings to mind the three "pillars" of the Christian church: James, Cephas and John (Galatians 2:9) and the twelve apostles. Of course, the numbers three and twelve appear frequently in Masonic rituals. In the Scottish Rite lodge the Master and the two Wardens are called the "lights" of the Lodge. The Royal Arch meets under the banners of the twelve tribes of Israel, etc.

An interesting passage is the following: "They [the members of the community] will be a precious cornerstone". This sentence recalls verses 16-17 in chapter 28 of Isaiah: "Behold, I lay a stone in Zion, a tested stone, a precious cornerstone for a sure foundation... I shall make justice a measuring line and righteousness the plumb line".

In Masonic initiation, the neophyte is placed in a particular position within the lodge and told that he is regarded as the cornerstone of the ideal Temple we are building. Furthermore, an entire Masonic degree (Mark Master) refers specifically to the cornerstone.

The measuring line in verse 17 is no other than a ruler, or it can be taken as representing the level, while the plumb line is the perpendicular. Both symbols of the Wardens.

After the Council meetings that ended with public confession and a new collective blessing to the newly initiated, they devoted themselves body and soul to the Great Work, to fulfill the congregation's statutes (Numbers 15:15: "The community is to have the same rules ... this is a lasting ordinance for the generations to come").

The Masters inculcated in their disciples mental discipline so that they could distinguish between good and evil, between lights and darkness (cf. 1 Kings 3:9: 'So give your servant a discerning heart to govern your people and to distinguish between right and wrong').

They also taught the principles of morality, tolerance and human solidarity. These are mainstays of Masonic teachings. The masters also inculcated liberal and democratic ideas, to walk the path of honor and justice, to defend the innocent and the downtrodden, to protect the widow and the orphan, and above all, to assist the needy.

All these are precisely the virtues closest to the hearts of Masons.

They also taught to dedicate themselves to work, combining individual effort with meditation and study, to achieve a high level of wisdom within a fraternal and just society. The members of the sect were educated in the art of meditation, reflecting on the meaning of life and the notion of loving one's neighbor.

The initiates, whose ages varied between 25 and 50 years, learned to "love justice and abhor evil".

They regarded themselves as heirs to the priest kings, symbolized by Melchizedek and Solomon. Some, like John the Baptist, made a vow as Nazirites. They must not be confused with the Nazarenes, those natives of Nazareth.

The Nazirite (from "nazir": separated or consecrated) consecrated himself fully to pious practices during a given period of time; he then abstained from wine or any fermented drink, did not eat grapes or raisins, did not shave or cut his hair, and could not come near a corpse, not even of his closest family. When his period of separation ended, he had to come to the entrance of the Tabernacle and present an offering to the priest. Then, the Nazirite cut his hair, could drink wine and bathe himself.

The Zadoquite Document contains a special section on the functions of the "mefaqueaj" or "Supervisor". The Hebrew word "mefaqueaj" is the exact equivalent of the Greek "episkopos", which is the origin of the word "bishop". The Supervisor was charged with educating the people, and make them understand the works of God. He had to explain in detail the history of the past and show to them the same compassion that a father shows to his children. He also had to examine each neophyte regarding his conduct, intelligence, strength, courage and possessions, to give him the appropriate rank.

His function was, in great measure, equivalent to that of the Wardens in a Masonic Lodge.

Finally, I would like to mention that some Jewish writers maintain that a section of the Essenes was called the Banaim, that is, the builders. It is not known why they were called with that name, but there is a reference in the Talmud that "the Masters in Israel are Builders (banaim)".

From all this, we shouldn't jump to the conclusion that Masonry may be a successor of the Essenes. The points of coincident we have noted are significant, but do not prove filiation. What does appear evident is that both the Essenes and the speculative Masons obeyed certain norms of conduct shared by all human beings who have reached a certain stage of spiritual development.

The writer Aldous Huxley, in his book The Perennial Philosophy, presents a good argument to demonstrate the coincidence of mystic traditions in different times and cultures.

The Dead Sea manuscripts are much more extensive than what I have described here. There are interesting passages about the end of time, Biblical commentaries, hymns of praise, and much more.

My purpose has been to focus only on some aspects of coincidence with Masonic rituals, particularly the Ancient and Accepted Scottish Rite, that has received and kept major influence from esoteric traditions, alchemy and Cabbala.

Freemasonry was not born in one piece, like the goddess Athena, but rather developed in an evolutionary process, absorbing symbols and legends from various sources. The Essenes, though distant in time and space, appear to have been one of the remote precursors of our Royal Art.

Bibliography:

The Holy Bible.
Josephus, Flavius, Antiquities and Wars of the Jews.
Gaster, Theodor H., The Dead Sea Scriptures.
Luria, Ben-Zion, Meguilat Hanejoshet Mimidbar Yehuda (In Jebrew: TheCopper Scroll of the Judean Desert), Jerusalem, 1963.
Vermes, Geza, The Dead Sea Scrolls in English, 3rd ed., London, Penguin, 1990.
Sukenik, Eliezer, Otzar Hameguilot Hagnuzot (in Hebrew: Collection of the Hidden Scrolls).
Sussman, Ayala and Ruth Peled, Scrolls from the Dead Sea, Library of Congress, Washington, 1993.
Wise, Michael, Martin Abegg, Jr. and Edward Cook, The Dead Sea Scrolls, Harper, 1996.
Wynn Wescott, W., "Freemasonry and its relation to the Essenes", Ars Quatuor Coronatorum, Vol. 28 (1915), pp. 67-79.

Chapter 12

KING SOLOMON'S QUARRIES

Me'arat Tzedkiyahu, or Zedekiah's Cave, more commonly known as the Quarries of King Solomon, is a deep cavern, opening beneath the wall of the Old City of Jerusalem, and extending for hundreds of meters under the surface of the city in the direction of the Temple Mount.

The cave's entrance, which had become lost in the course of centuries of vandalism and neglect, was rediscovered in 1854. The opening lies at the base of the wall, some hundred meters north of the Damascus Gate and near King Herod's Gate. It is one of the most extensive caverns in Israel, measuring about 220 meters in length and some 900 meters in circumference. The discrepancy between these figures is explained by the cave's numerous side chambers.

According to tradition, the cave extends all the way to the plain of Jericho. Zedekiah, the last king of Judah, is said to have fled through the cavern when Jerusalem fell into the hands of Nebuchadnezzar, the Babylonian king, in the summer of 587 BCE. This is obviously a tale of imagination. It was Josephus Flavius, the great Jewish historian of the first century, who for the first time called it the 'Royal Cavern', later to become known as 'King Solomon's Quarries.' Whatever truth there may be in that designation, the fact remains that the cave did serve as a quarry for building stone, and the half-hewn blocks of stone still in place give testimony to this effect.

The type of stone found in the case is the white limestone known locally as melech or 'Royal' stone. It is very good for building purposes and, although it is not particularly hard, it does not flake. Very large blocks of this stone can be quarried.

The rock at the cave opening is of a different kind, called mizzi-helou or 'sweet' stone. It is easily worked through its striations, which prevent it being used in large blocks. A third kind of stone known as mizzi-ahmar or 'red' stone is also found in the cave.

The cave is divided into chambers, separated by broad columns left by the quarriers to support the roof. Traces of the technique used by the ancient masons can be observed. Broad slits were hewn along the wall and dry wooden wedges were driven into them. Water was then poured over the wedges. The expanding wood eventually cracked the stone along the slit. This primitive method of quarrying is quite effective and is still used in many parts of the world.

As the quarries in the cave are quite close to the Temple Mount (Mount Moriah, site of Solomon's Temple) and to the City of David, even very large stone blocks could have been transported there. The limestone hardens when exposed to sunlight and the elements. Obviously, it would have been simpler to use this quarry rather than bringing up heavy stones from Jaffa, via the winding road uphill to Jerusalem.

An interesting possibility was raised in this connection by Bro. William C. Blaine,[1] who noted that the depth of the quarry would prevent any noise reaching the site of the Temple on Mount Moriah. This would explain verse 6:7 in the first Book of Kings: 'In building the Temple, only blocks dressed in the quarry were used, and no hammer, chisel or any other iron tool was heard at the Temple site while it was being built.'

In some of the chambers, deep pits remain at places where the stone was taken out in large quantities. These are now fenced around to prevent the accidental fall of visitors. Every few yards, inches were carved in the walls for oil lamps. Traces of soot can still be seen above some. Huge, half-cut rectangular shapes of stone, nearly ready to be removed, pose an intriguing question, why the workmen left so suddenly, leaving the valuable stones in place.

Another legend is that deep within the cave are hidden the treasures of the Temple, hidden by the priests when the Roman armies under Titus were besieging the city.[2]

A few years after the cave's entrance was discovered, this was the place where the first recorded Masonic ceremony performed in Palestine took place, in 1868. The meeting was organized by Most Worshipful Brother Robert Morris, Past Grand Master of the Grand Lodge of Kentucky, who had come to the Holy Land in search of traces of Freemasonry from King Solomon's time. Rob Morris, as he signed his name, found only a few isolated Masons living in Palestine, which was then part of the Ottoman Empire. Morris met in Jerusalem Captain (later Sir) Charles Warren, the British Military Engineer and Archeologist, who had been sent by the Palestine Exploration Fund to conduct explorations in Jerusalem. He later became the first Master of Quatuor Coronati Lodge N 2076 in London, the premier Lodge of Research in the world. By chance, a British naval unit, H.M.S. Lord Clyde, arrived in Jaffa for a brief visit. The captain and several officers were Masons. Morris invited them all to a ceremony in the Secret Monitor degree, performed in the cavern on 13 May 1868. Others who took part in the ceremony were Noureddin Effendi, the Turkish Governor of Jaffa, who was a member of the Amitie Clemente Lodge of Paris and held the 28 Degree in the Scottish Rite; Henry Peterman, Consul of Prussia in Jerusalem, four Christian Americans then living in Jaffa, and the American Vice-Consul, R. Beardsley, of Elkhart, Indiana.

Local Masons continued to use the quarry occasionally, particularly to perform the Mark Master degree, for which the cave is remarkably well suited. This tradition was broken in 1948, when the Old City of Jerusalem was captured by Jordan's Arab Legion. Fearing that some of the tunnels running from the main chamber might lead to the Jewish city, the Jordanian authorities sealed the entrance to the cave. Only in 1967, when the Holy City was again reunited, and after the cave had been made safe for visitors, could Masonic ceremonies at the quarries be resumed.

On 3 July 1969, this was the venue chosen to perform a solemn ceremony consecrating the Supreme Royal Arch Chapter of the State of Israel. The ceremony was conducted by Most Excellent Companion the Earl of Galloway, First Grand Principal of the Supreme Grand Royal Arch Chapter of Scotland and Sovereign Grand Commander of the Supreme Council of the Scottish Rite for Scotland.[3]

Beginning in 1979, frequent groups of Masons from England, Scotland, South Africa and the United States have come to Israel on Masonic pilgrimages, the highlight of which is the performance of the Mark Master degree in King Solomon's Quarries. Usually, the visiting brethren then participate in an Excellent Master degree ('Passing the Veils') which is not worked in England.

Chapter Notes

1 Blaine, William C., "King Solomon's Quarries", The Israel Scottish Rite, Vol. 3, N 1, December 1973, p. 23.
2 Brunton, Roy, "King Solomon's Quarries", The Israel Scottish Rite, N 7, January-March 1969, p. 13.
3 Elman, Joe, "A Lodge in Solomon's Quarries", The Israel Scottish Rite, N 5, June 1972, p. 190.

Chapter 13

SOME SEPHARDIC JEWS IN FREEMASONRY

First mentions in England

In England, where the Jews had been expelled by King Edward I in the year 1290, some "secret" Jews entered the country surreptitiously, under the appearance of being Spanish or Portuguese Catholics. They attended mass in the embassies of Spain, Portugal and France, but observed Jewish traditions in their homes. These Jews were tolerated because of their financial and mercantile contacts with the rest of Europe, and by their assistance in extending the commercial interests of England throughout the world. Enjoying the more liberal environment prevailing in England and Holland, some Jews gradually revealed themselves as such. In 1655, the Sephardic Rabbi Menasseh ben Israel (also known as Manoel Dias Soeiro, 1604-1657) from Amersterdam, submitted a petition to Oliver Cromwell to allow the official residence of Jews in England. No record has been found of the result of this demarche, but a small congregation of Sephardim was officially recognized by King Charles II in 1664, after the Restoration of the Stuart monarchy. [1]

Thus, the new Israelite congregation in England was composed almost exclusively of Sephardim. The first Jews who received nobility titles in England also were Sephardim: Solomon de Medina (c. 1650-1730) and Sir Moses Montefiore (1784-1885), who was knighted in 1837 and made a baronet in 1846.

It is not surprising, then, that the first known Jewish Mason, dating from 1716 (one year *before* the creation of the first Grand Lodge) was an English Sephardi: Francis Francia, also known as the "Jacobite Jew". He was tried and later exonerated from an accusation of high treason. In an English newspaper of 1877, recounting this incident, Francia is called a Mason.

In 1732 another Jew, Edward Rose, was initiated in a lodge presided by Daniel Delvalle, 'eminent Jew snuff merchant' as characterized in a report in the *Daily Post* of 22 September 1732. Without doubt Delvalle must have preceded Rose by several years, to have reached the high position of Master of the lodge. Furthermore, Bro. Mathias Levy, in an article entitled 'Jews as Freemasons' published in *The Jewish Chronicle* in 1898, claims that the initiation took place 'in the presence of Jews and non-Jews". These other Jews present must have been masons themselves, initiated at an earlier date.

Other Sephardi brethren appear in the records of the 18th century. The register of brethren of 1725 includes Israel Segalas and Nicholas Abrahams. Earlier still, in 1721, appear the names of Nathan Blanch (perhaps his original name was Blanco) and John Hart, though it is not certain they were Jews. [2]

Several Jews are listed as Grand Stewards in Anderson's *New Book of Constitutions* (1738): Solomon Mendez in 1732, Meyer Shamberg, M.D. in 1735, Benjamin Da Costa in 1737 and Isaac Barrett, Joseph Harris, Samuel Lowman and Moses Mendez in 1737-1738. Most of them were Sephardim.

The first recorded Jewish officer of the Antients' Grand Lodge was David Lyon, Grand Tyler (1760-63), later promoted to Grand Pursuivant (1764-65). In the Moderns' Grand Lodge, the first was Moses Isaac Levi (alias Ximenes), appointed both Junior and Senior Grand Warden in 1785. That same year John Paiba, who had held some office since 1779, was appointed Grand Sword Bearer.[3]

Two other English Jews are famous in Masonic history, because of having been arrested by the Inquisition in Lisbon and condemned as Masons (not because of being crypto-Jews!). They were later released and related their experiences. The first was John Coustos (1703-?), arrested in 1740, about whom numerous papers have been published.[4] Some historians express doubts about his Judaism, but in his paper already quoted, Bro. Shaftesley bring up many indications pointing to the fact that "John Coustos, if he was not of Jewish origin, gave a very good imitation of it". [5]

The second case is that of Hyppolito da Costa (1774-1823), who, although a professed Christian himself, belonged to a renowned family of Sephardic Jews in Portugal, England

and the West Indies. At the time, there were almost two dozen Da Costas or Mendez da Costas in the diamond trade. Da Costa, whose full name was Hyppolito Joseph da Costa Pereira Furtado de Mendoca was initiated in the Lodge of the Nine Muses in 1807 and joined the Lodge of Antiquity in 1808. He was a friend of the Dukes of Sussex and Leinster, and eventually reached the high office of Provincial Grand Master for Rutland. In 1898, AQC published a note about Ben Da Costa, a Past Master of Friars Lodge and Preceptor of the Israel Lodge of Instruction (N÷ 205), who was undoubtedly Jewish and claimed to be a relative of Hyppolito da Costa. [6]

On 23 December 1731, only 14 years after the foundation of the Premier Grand Lodge, Lodge N÷ 84 raised columns in London, at the Daniel Coffee House on Lombard Street. Among the brethren listed were several Jews: Salomon Mendez, Abraham Ximenez, Jacob Alvarez, Abraham de Medina, Benjamin Adolphus and Isaac Baruch. That is to say, out of six, five were Sephardim. They constituted a fifth of the total membership of the Lodge, that numbered 29 brethren. [7]

Sir Moses Montefiore (1784-1885)

Montefiore was born in Livorno, Italy. He was an active Mason, having been initiated in Moira Lodge in 1812. His brother-in-law, Nathan Meyer Rothschild, had been initiated ten years earlier in the Emulation Lodge. Montefiore and Rothschild had married sisters, daughters of Levi Barent Cohen.

He was knighted in 1837 by Queen Victoria. That same year Benjamin Disraeli was elected to Parliament as a Tory.

In August of 1840, together with the French Lawyer and high-ranking mason Adolphe Cremieux (1796-1880), he led a delegation to Turkey and secured the release of the captives of the Damascus blood libel. He also persuaded the sultan of Turkey to issue a edict forbidding the circulation of blood libels.

In 1863, supported by the British government, Sir Moses Montefiore petitioned the sultan of Morocco, Muhammad IV, to guarantee the safety of Morocco's Jews. His efforts were successful.

A year later, in 1864, he intervened in order to gain the release of rabbi Meir Leib ben Jehiel Michael Malbin, chief rabbi of Bucharest, who had been wrongly accused of disloyalty to the authorities.

Sir Moses Montefiore

His connection with Eretz Israel is well known, and his horse carriage, as well as his wind-mill can still be seen in Jerusalem.

Upon reaching the ripe age of 80 years, "*gil hagvurah*" in Hebrew tradition, English Jewish Masons founded in 1864 the *Montefiore Lodge* N 1017 in London. Later, in 1888, a second Montefiore lodge (N 753) was founded in Glasgow and in 1996 a third lodge, *Montefiore Lodge of Installed Masters N 78,* was consecrated in Tel Aviv.

Rabbi Leon Templo

Rabbi Jacob Jehudah Jacob Leon (1603-1675), known as Leon Templo, deserves special mention. In 1675 he brought to London models of the Jerusalem Temple and the Tabernacle, which he had previously exhibited in Amsterdam. Leon Templo was also an expert in heraldry. His work so impressed Laurence Dermott, the first Grand Secretary of the Grand Lodge of Antients, that he took a design by Leon Templo as the basis for the coat of arms of the Antients. When the two Grand Lodges of England merged to form the present United Grand Lodge (1813), this design was incorporated in its coat of arms. The model of the Templo built by Leon Templo was again exhibited by Bro. M.P. de Castro, who claimed to be a relative of the builder.

An interesting historical question is the possible existence of a Masonic organization in Amsterdam in which Jews were allowed to join before the creation of the Premier Grand Lodge of London. There are two indications that point to that possibility.

Dermott, in the second edition of *Ahiman Rezon* - the Book of Constitutions of the Antients - published in 1764, called Templo "the famous and learned Hebrewist [sic], Architect and brother". Historians have generally dismissed the 'brother' appellation as either an error or a friendly sobriquet. However, we do know that Leon came originally from Livorno. His daughter, Elisebah, was married to Jacob Yehuda Leon, also characterized as "from Livorno". A flourishing Jewish community lived in that Italian city that became a refuge for Sephardic Jews fleeing from the Spanish Inquisition, and who returned to practicing Judaism openly. The Jews of Livorno maintained close links with other Sephardic communities in North Africa, particularly Tunis.

Livorno

Livorno was an important center of masonic activity in Italy. To give an example, among 34 lodges active in Italy between 1815 and 1860, no less than 19 were located in Livorno, that is, over 50% of all Italian lodges.[8] A document from the lodge *Les Amis de la Parfaite Union* dated 3 May 1797 lists nine Jewish members from a total of 56.[9]

The presence of Jews in Livorno dates from the 16th century. Jewish bankers were already present in the duchy of Tuscany when Cosimo I declared the city a free port in 1548.

On June 10, 1593, duke Ferdinand I de Medici, issued *La Livornana*, letters patent addressed to "Levantines (i.e. Easterners), Spaniards, Portuguese, Germans and Italians", but in reality intended for the Jews of those countries, granting them full religious liberty, amnesty for crimes committed previously, and the opportunity for Marranos to return to Judaism unmolested and to receive Tuscan citizenship, subject to the approval of the heads of the community (the *Massari*). The community had a large degree of autonomy and were exempt from wearing the yellow Jewish badge.

The Medici rulers wanted to develop Livorno as their main port of trade. The Jewish community in Livorno grew rapidly, from a few hundred in the late 1500's to about 5000 in 1689. The city became an important entrepot for trade between Atlantic and Northern ports and those of the Mediterranean and the Near East. In 1765, one third of Livorno's 150 commercial houses were Jewish-owned.[10] In 1650 Issac Gabai established a printing press that rivaled that of Venice in the production of valuable Hebrew books. The community was so prosperous that, at the urging of Colbert, chief minister of Luis XIV of France, the king invited the Jews of Livorno to some and settle in Marseilles.[11]

Ménasseh Ben Israël

Menasseh Ben Israel

Rabbi Hayim Joseph David Azulai, who lived in Livorno the last 30 years of his life, wrote a travel book in Hebrew, in which he recounts an incident that occurred to him in 1754 in Tunis, when the son of the Kaid (Moslem governor) of the city asked him, in the middle of the night, if he could kill a group of Jews from Livorno who belonged to "the sect of Franc Masons". In his answer, the Rabbi (who ordered not to touch them) confessed having heard of the Masons, but that they did not have a bad reputation, but were like "a comedy". [12]

Certainly, the date is much later than the period of Leon Templo, who had died in 1675, almost 80 years earlier, but we have here irrefutable evidence that in Livorno existed an active group of Jewish Masons, and we cannot dismiss out of hand the possibility that a proto-masonic organization open to Jews existed in Livorno, Amsterdam and possibly other places at the end of the 17th century.

Another incident pointing to the presence of Jewish Masons in North Africa is mentioned by Bro. Shaftesley in his paper already quoted, taking it from Robert Freke Gould's *History of Freemasonry*: "in a minute of the Stewards" Lodge of March 1764, in connection with Laurence Dermott's great linguistic attainments, "an Arabian Mason having petitioned for relief, the Grand Secretary [Dermott] conversed with him in the Hebrew language". The use of Hebrew and not Arabic demonstrates that the "Arabian" must have been a Jewish Mason from North Africa.

The Campanal enigma

The second indication in this respect is the case of Campanal (or Campanall) in Newport, Rhode Island. In the Winter, 1967 issue of *The Royal Arch Mason* (US), a letter was printed from Comp. Samuel W. Freedman of Wilmington, Delaware, entitled "Did Jews Introduce Masonry in America?". The letter says (in part) as follows:

"While touring New England this past summer, I stopped in Rhode Island where I visited the Touro Synagogue, which has been designated as a national shrine by the United States Government because it is the oldest synagogue on the American continent.[13] In a historical pamphlet, recently put out by the Touro Synagogue Congregation, I ran across a note that is rather interesting. I am sending to you a photocopy of one of the pages in the pamphlet:

> 'The first documentary evidence of the presence of Jews in Newport dates from 1658. In that year the document reads: **"Wee mett att ye House of Mordecai Campanall and after Synagog Wee gave Abm Moses the degrees of Maconrie".** This not only points to the early settlement of Jews in Rhode Island, but it is the basis for the theory ¾ which has been questioned by some ¾ that the craft of Masonry was first introduced into America through the early Jewish settlers in Rhode Island, who seemed to have worked the degrees after religious services which were held in private houses'.

"Upon returning home a chain of thought started in my mind, wondering whether there isn't more of a basis to the speculative Masonry we practice than we think. The Jews who came to Newport were either Spanish or Portuguese, who first went to Brazil and Curacao in South America from where they came to Newport."

In a further issue of The Royal Arch Mason[14], Bro. Norman G. Mccullough adds new information on the subject:

"In the Book *The History of Freemasonry and Concordant Orders* (Stillson and Hugan, 1904), I find a most interesting explanation. Division VIII under 'First Glimpses in North America,' indicates that the second vestige of Masonry in this country, is described in Peterson's History of Rhode Island (1835, p. 101). The author informs us that:

"In the spring of 1657, Mordecai Campanall, Moses Packeckoe, Levi, and others, in all 15 families, arrived at Newport from Holland. They brought with them the three first degrees of Masonry, and worked them in the house of Campanall, and continued to do so, and their successors, to the year 1742."

"The statement was said to have been made on the authority of documents in the possession of N.H. Gould, Esq., at the time of the publication of the history. It came to the notice of Grand Master William S. Gardner, who was greatly astonished at the information, and immediately set about to investigate. He applied to Brother Gould, of Newport, Rhode Island, who was then an active member of the Supreme Council, Ancient and Accepted Scottish Rite (Northern Jurisdiction). Gould replied that the statement was founded upon a dilapidated document found among the effects of a distant relative of his. It had been exposed to alternate humidity and heat and was so broken and brittle that it could not be daguerreotyped. All that could be made out was that in 1656 or 1658:

"Wee mett att ye House off Mordecai Campannall and after Synagog Wee gave Abm Moses the degrees of Maconrie."

"Grand Master Gardiner was not satisfied with the evidence and declared that it was 'almost impossible to treat this story with the attention which the subject demands'".

"In Rhode Island, Grand Master Doyle commented on Gould's letter:

"It would seem the only authority in his possession is a document showing that in 1656 or 1658 somebody met some other persons at some house in Newport, and 'gave Abm Moses the degrees of Masonrie'. This may have occurred then and there, just as stated; but, if so, it is no authority for the statement that a lodge of Masons existed then in Newport, or that there was any legal Masonic authority for the work done, or that any other person was ever legally made a Mason in Newport between 1658 and 1742."

"It is certain, however, that the tradition has long been perpetuated that Masons made their appearance in Rhode Island about that time. In Weeden's recently published *Economic and Social History of New England*, under the date 1658, the author says: 'The commerce of Newport was extending. The wealthy Jews, who contributed so much to it, afterward, appear now. It is said that 15 families came in from Holland this year, bringing with their goods and mercantile skill the first three degrees of Freemasonry".

Thus Bro. Mccullough. Clearly, the brethren who came to Rhode Island were Sephardic Jews. Campannall is a corruption of Campanal ("bell ringer" in Spanish), and Packeckoe is probably a corruption of Pacheco, a common Spanish name. Levi is also common among Sephardim. Bro. Sidney Kase, in his article "Freemasonry and the Jews" [15] mentions that Campanal's original name was Campanelli. The Italian form suggests that he came originally from Italy, possibly from Livorno.

From another source, we learn that Abraham Campanal, from Newport, Rhode Island, evidently a descendant of Mordechai but who had been raised as a Christian, came to Curacao in 1718 to be circumcised and return to Judaism. Unfortunately, he died after the operation, probably from infection, and this resulted in a probibition for a certain period to circumcise Christians.[16]

All this is inconclusive, but it is certainly suggestive. A formal lodge may not have existed in Rhode Island in the late 17th century, but Masons are known to have assembled in what is called a "moot" lodge before receiving a warrant from a regular Grand Lodge (which in any case did not exist at that time). It appears to this author that, starting from the preconceived premise that no Masonry could have existed in Holland before the 18th century, historians have tended to dismiss the cases of Leon Templo and Campanal our of hand. Nevertheless, if we accept this possibility, new avenues of research are opened before us.

To end this relation, I shall mention that the first Jew initiated in America was also a Sephardi. In 1733, Moses Nunis (whose original name was probably Moises Nunez) was initiated in Georgia at the age of 34 years. He died in 1787 and was buried with a Masonic funeral.[17]

And finally, a note about Chile, a country where Freemasonry has played an outstanding role in promoting tolerance and education. The first regular Masonic lodge in that country that worked in the national language, Spanish, was created at the initiative of a Sephardic Jew, Manuel de Lima y Sola, in the year 1853. He was also the promoter of the creation of the Grand Lodge of Chile, in the year 1862.

Chapter Notes

1 Shaftesley, John F., "Jews in English Freemasonry in the 18th and 19th Centuries", *Ars Quatuor Coronatorum (AQC)*, Vol. 92 (1979), pp.25-63.
2 Shaftesley, *op.cit.*
3 Shaftesley, *op. cit.* p. 42
4 See, *inter alia*, McLeod, W., "John Coustos: his Lodges and his Book", *AQC*, Vol. 92 (1979), pp. 113-147. Vatcher, S., "John Coustos and the Portuguese Inquisition", *AQC*, Vol. 81 (1968), pp. 9-87. The original documentation in Portuguese appears transcribed into Spanish in Ferrer Benimeli, Jose A., *Masoneria, Iglesia e Ilustracion: un conflicto ideologico-politico-religioso. Vol. I: Las Bases de un Conflicto (1700-1739)*, Madrid, 1975 pp. 301-326.
5 Shaftesley, *op. cit.*, p. 27
6 Shaftesley, *ibidem*.
Shaftesley, *op. cit.* p. 37
For instance, Shane, Lewis A., "Jacob Judah Leon of Amsterdam (1602-1675) and his models of the Temple of Salomon and the Tabernacle", AQC, Vol. 96, p. 146
7 Shaftesley, *op. cit.*, p. 37.
8 Polo Friz, Luigi, "Logge in Italia dal 1816 al 1870", *Massoneria Oggi*, Year V, No. 4, August-September 1998, p. 27.
9 Stolper, Ed., "Contributo allo studio della massoneria italiana nell'era napoleonica", *Rivista Massonica*, September 1977.
10 *Encyclopaedia Judaica*, Jerusalem 1971, Vol. 10, p. 1572.
11 Heller, Marvin H., "Jedidiah ben Isaac Gabai and the first decade of Hebrew printing in Livorno", *Los Muestros*, Brussels, No. 33, December 1998.
12 *Sefer Ma'agal Tov Hashalem* (Book of the Good Complete Circuit), reproduced by Mekitzei Nirdamin, Jerusalem, 5694

(1934), p. 64.

13 The Touro synagogue started on 1759 and concluded on 1763, was built by Isaac Abraham Touro, a Rabbi who had come from Amsterdam in 1760.

14 Reprinted in *Haboneh Hahofshi* (Journal of the Grand Lodge of Israel) , Vol. 43, No. 1-2, April 1976, pp. 19-21.

15 *The Philalethes*, Vol. XLII, N÷4, August 1989, pp. 6-10, 23.

16 Arbell, Mordechai, "Return to Jadaism, the Circumcisers (Mohalim) of Curacao",
Los Muestros, No. 28, September 1997, pp. 23-24.

17 Kase, Sidney, "Freemasonry and the Jews", *The Philalethes*, August, 1989, p. 8.

Chapter 14

PROJECTING THE VALUES OF FREEMASONRY IN SOCIETY

If there is something in which the majority of contemporary thinkers are in agreement, are that we are experiencing a world crisis. As somebody remarked: 'God is dead, communism has failed, and I myself don't feel so good.'

There is talk of a crisis of values, the end of ideology, the oil crisis, the ozone crisis, the Aids crisis, the economic crisis. The word crisis is in crisis because of overuse.

The fact is, whether the situation of crisis exists or not, the sensation of crisis undoubtedly does, and this is almost the same thing.

It is not only anxiety due to uncertainty about the future. The malaise affecting us has deep roots, and perhaps less conscious as well. The angst of our time is comparable to the sensation of somebody who is sliding down a slope without being able to reduce his speed, or seeing what lies behind the next hillock. Worse still, he doesn't know why he is there in the first place.

The 'future shock' brilliantly predicted by writer Alvin Toffler a few years ago is no longer in the future but a daily reality. Knowledge acquired with great effort in the course of years becomes outdated and irrelevant in a matter of weeks. No sooner have we learned to use a new computer program, when another one appears, better than the previous one (so it is claimed), certainly different.

The problems at work, in the family, in society, are become more severe, the demands more stringent. We are sick of novelties.

As another millennium begins, we observe the growing chasm between our ever accelerating technological progress and the stagnation - if not backsliding - in the moral and intellectual development of the human race. We should not be surprised, then, if apocalyptic movements and fanatical cults appear here and there, with increasing frequency.

To speak of the new Middle Ages has become hackneyed. Berdiaeff, the Russian philosopher and mystic, writing after World War I, already gave this title to one of his books. The death of God was proclaimed by Nietszche over a century ago. So let us leave aside these shopworn concepts, and within the limited space of this chapter, let us examine instead in what way we might alleviate our condition, even if perfect solutions are not within our reach.

Better to light a candle than to curse the night, says an old Chinese aphorism. This is precisely my intention. It could not be otherwise, taking into consideration the optimist and meliorist vision of the human condition implicit in our Masonic ideology.

Freemasonry proclaims the possibility of improving society, starting with the betterment of the individual. Hence the vital importance our Order assigns to education, as the means of advancement and rectification, both of the individual and of society as a whole. Education is the best antidote against prejudice and intolerance. Education is the most efficient form of charity.

However, education, commented Krause, is something most people receive, many transmit, but very few have. The problem, as with so many other philosophical questions, lies in the definition of our terms. If education is conceived as simply a transfer of information, we will fall into the condition observed by Trevelyan: a great many people know how to read, but are incapable of recognizing what is worth reading.

Condorcet, in 1790, clearly indicated the ends of public education, and the first objective he postulated is the following: 'Offer all individuals of the human species the means to provide for their needs, ensure their welfare, know and exercise their rights, understand and fulfill their duties. Please note: not a word about mere accumulation of knowledge. We could hardly improve on this definition, even today.

Nowadays, data is obtained with utmost ease. It's enough to have access to a computer terminal, and the whole world of information is at your fingertips. If we suffer, it is not because we lack information, but because we are overwhelmed by it. We have a surfeit of information. The importance of education is precisely the acquisition of the capacity to judge, to categorize, to personally classify and evaluate the quality of the information received, not only from the factual, but also from the ethical and teleological standpoints.

Particularly in our present world, submerged as we are in a maelstrom of stimuli and distractions that pull us apart from the essential, where, as noted by Umberto Eco, mass media not only transmit an ideology, but have become an ideology themselves, the spirit of serene and academic examination is the last refuge of the thinking man.

The university thus becomes the fortress of Humanism, the forum where all ideas are brandished and debated within the greatest freedom, restricted only by the freedom of others. That is as it should be, though unfortunately in some universities 'politically correct' thought has shackled free discourse.

Free discourse is the function that Freemasonry must assume in its Lodges, and that is only one parallel among many that link both institutions, University and Masonry.

This may be an opportune moment to underline the fact that Masonry, as a social and historical phenomenon, must be studied as an integral part of the history of ideas, while its philosophy, without question, belongs in the stream of philosophical thought of Western civilization and is inseparable from it.

The same refreshing and humanistic impulse introduced in Europe during the Renaissance, which led to the study of the classics and brought about a rebirth of architecture, that beginning with Bacon established the bases of the inductive and experimental method of scientific research, would eventually lead to the present development of science and technology. This creative impulse resulted in the foundation of the Royal Society of England in 1660, the first body devoted to scientific research, and on the other hand, it found expression in the creation of the premier Grand Lodge in London, on June 24, 1717. It should not surprise us to learn that many scientific and philosophical personalities of the time were active in creating both institutions.

Putting together science and philosophy is not accidental. The rots of modern science lie in Renaissance philosophy, and 'Natural Philosophy' was an early name for physical science.

Freemasonry is intimately connected with the social changes and the development of ideas in Europe in the 17th and 18th centuries. No serious study of the beginnings of Speculative Masonry, for example, can ignore the role played in English society at the time by the important influx of Huguenots, fleeing France after the Mt. Bartholomew massacre. According to one author, the most important single English contributor to the Enlightenment was John Locke, who believed in religious tolerance and was in almost unbroken contact with French-speaking Protestants from 1675 until his death in 1704. A Huguenot, John Theophilus Desaguliers (1683-1744), who was a scientist of note, member of the Royal Society and friend of Newton, had an important influence on the beginnings of English Freemasonry, serving as its third Grand Master (1719) and later as Deputy Grand Master for several years.

Any serious study of Masonic philosophy must address the Rosicrucian phenomenon in the 17th and 18th centuries, the development of Hebrew Cabala and its Christian offshoot, the different semi-secret and semi-occult groups that flourished in Europe from the end of the Middle Ages until the Victorian age, from Dante's Fideli D'amore, through Baron Tschoudy's mock-Templars and down to the Golden Dawn created by Wynn Wescott and MacGregor Mathers in the last decades of the 19th century.

On the other hand, a study of European or Western philosophy that ignores Freemasonry is also incomplete. A writer of the stature of Lessing (called the first German playwright of importance) could author the Masonic Dialogs, and poets such as Kipling and Burns wrote many masonic poems in glowing terms.

However, let me return to the theme proposed at the beginning of this chapter. Having observed the prevailing malaise of our 'global village', and having established the validity and place of masonic philosophy within an academic framework, we should now focus our attention on the principles of Masonry, on the one hand, and in what way they can be applied in order to assuage, as far as possible, the existential anguish of contemporary man.

An objection could be advanced, that such a study is pointless, because we would be guilty of hubris if we were to pretend that the discussions held within a Lodge or any other Masonic context could really affect the course of events in our society.

However, the pen is mightier than the sword. Men pass away, and their memory fades until only a distant reflection of their presence remains with us. Who can remember offhand the Nobel prize winners of a decade ago? But ideas live forever, embodied in words capable of stirring our heart no less today than centuries ago.

What are those ideas, transmitted by our Craft, that we believe capable of improving the world? I can only graze the surface of our subject. I will try, then, to summarize Masonic teachings in two fundamental principles, like the two columns at the entrance to King Solomon's Temple. These may not be the same ideas enunciated elsewhere by other Masonic authors, but I will ask you to bear with me for a moment.

In my opinion, the first fundamental principle that sustains our institution, more important than charity, mutual assistance, tolerance, and all other virtues that we cultivate, is simply personal responsibility. To Cain's anguished question, resounding from century to century even to our day, 'Am I my brother's keeper?', we give a ringing and unequivocal reply: 'Yes, I am!'

Let me explain a little further. We want to improve the world, eradicate poverty, ignorance, disease and war, but improving the world is a huge project, depending not only on us, but on many others, as well as a multitude of factors over which we have no influence whatsoever.

On the other hand, our personal improvement depends only on our personal resolve. It's our decision and nobody else's. Every human being is capable of polishing his imperfections, restraining his bad impulses, developing positive inclinations, without requesting anybody's permission, under any circumstances, in any place and time. If we want to, we can be better.

Masonry gives us support, shows the way, stimulates and lends us the symbolic tools to make our task easier, but in the final account, we must wield the tools, each at his own pace, following his own music and way through life. That is personal responsibility.

The second principle, no less important than the first, is the possibility of finding a common ground, of working together, involving collaboration and developing feelings of fraternal affection among persons with the most diverse backgrounds, with different social and ethnic origins, speaking diverse languages, belonging to different cultures, religions and political factions. Despite all these enormous differences, which Freemasonry recognizes and accepts, it still insists in demonstrating that there is a common level of humanity that binds us all, a joint yearning toward that far distant goal that makes us fellow travelers on the road to truth. Our ideal is capable of surmounting all inequalities.

Working together, we develop our sentiments of Fraternity and Charity, Tolerance and Assistance. This great principle, which I might call Fraternal Cohesion, the possibility of establishing and developing links of sincere friendship among all men, is perhaps our greatest contribution to society, so often divided by class, religion and politics, not to speak of prejudice or blind hatred.

Fraternal Cohesion finds expression both in the spiritual and the material realms. In the spiritual, by the instant affective communication that develops between Masons who have never met before, and may never meet again. No less important, this bond grows within us, and the assistance lent to others miraculously creates in us a wealth of inner satisfaction. In the material, this principle finds expression in the many works of philanthropy and social benefit undertaken by Masons individually and institutionally throughout the world, often hidden under a veil of discretion.

The Mason is taught to give without causing offense to the less fortunate. This discretion has led to a situation where much of our charitable efforts are ignored by the world at large, or are attributed to other, non-Masonic sources. How many people know, for instance, that taken together, Masonic charities in the United States of America distribute over 3 million dollars every day? Children's hospitals, medical research, libraries, universities, cultural institutions of every kind benefit from Masonic largesse.

The same could be said, guarding the proportions, of Masonry in many other countries. Looking back at the depressing picture with which I started, we can see that Masonry can and does help, can and does make a difference.

How about our personal improvement? Masonry imposes on us a discipline of thought, a philosophical posture that demands rational examination of problems. Just as Marcus Aurelius had ever present the fragility of human existence, which led him to disdain the miseries of life, the Mason who has gone through the experience of symbolic death learns to face with serenity the tumultuous landscape of daily strife, the strident claims of the media, the hysterical demands of the merchants of ideologies. We treasure silence, and silence is the best antidote against confusion.

Secondly, we face the future with confidence and optimism. This is an imponderable factor, but one that subtly colors our way of looking at things and strengthens our resolve, sustaining a proactive rather than a passive stance.

Freemasonry's external action depends, of course, on local circumstances. Masons have fought for religious tolerance, universal education, the separation of church and state, the removal of social barriers of every kind.

Let me add a few words about Freemasonry in Israel. This, as you will see, has relevance for our analysis.

What characterizes Israeli Freemasonry, and has done so from its early beginnings at the end of the 19th century, is its ethnic and cultural diversity. Starting with the first Lodges, in Jaffa and Jerusalem, Arabs and Jews have always been working together in harmony, keeping alive the flame of brotherhood even in the most trying circumstances of religious and political strife.

Israel's Masonry is composed of a majority of Jews, and a strong proportion of Christian and Muslim Arabs, much greater than their demographic weight in the total population. This pluralist tradition has withstood wars, riots, terror and general bloodshed. Our Grand Lodge has three Sacred Volumes open on its altar: the Jewish Tanakh, the Christian New Testament and the Koran. Three Grand Chaplains have equal rank. The Grand Lodge Seal includes the cross, the crescent, the Star of David, all enclosed within square and compasses.

Israel gives direct and irrefutable testimony that Masonic ideals do work, and have proven their worth during scores of years of uninterrupted conflict.

This, moreover, is no isolated instance. I could give numerous examples taken from the history of other countries, showing the enlightened and beneficial influence of Freemasonry in reducing the pain and suffering of warfare.

Masonry operates through its members. The Institution in itself is apolitical and philosophical, but, as Professor Jorge Carvajal, Grand Master of Chile and Rector of La Republica University has remarked, the university does not operate patients or build bridges. And Masonry does not intervene directly in the life of the country, but both institutions make their effect felt through their graduates and individual members.

The influence of Freemasonry is not limited to what its members do themselves. The love of freedom, the lesson of tolerance learned in the course of Masonic activities, are inevitably reflected in the professional and family life of its members, in their dealings with others, their way of life as a whole. Their example spreads like ever widening circles of a wave and elicits favorable reactions in others, contributing to improve human relations, moderate extremism, control the passions. Whether a judge or an architect, a politician or a merchant, the influence of Freemasonry contributes to reinforce man's natural impulse to do good, seek the truth, help others and avoid excess.

I shall quote a few sentences from an article published in 1970 by Brother Pedro Fernandez Riffo, entitled 'Masonry and Axiology', that will illustrate by thesis.

After reviewing the different theories of values proposed by philosophers and their connection with Freemasonry, the author writes as follows: 'Freemasonry teaches us that the philosophical knowledge achieved must not remain, cannot remain simply theoretical knowledge. Masonry demands action in social life. It is all together a system of tasks.'

'Philosophy, as well, invites to action, because to act is to live, and philosophy is embedded in life itself... Let us remember Ortega y Gasset, for whom human life is a manner of doing philosophy.'

A related thought was briefly noted by Marcus Aurelius in one of his meditations: 'It's not a matter of discoursing about what a good man must be, but of being one.'

This, too, is Masonic philosophy. We trust in the actuality and effectiveness of our principles. We trust in the possibility of improving ourselves, and thereby improve the society in which we live. And we work diligently, here and now, for the realization of these objectives.

Human beings aspire to perfection, strive to become better, and if we create the conditions that will enable them to develop all their capacities, there is no limit to what can still be achieved. Freemasonry, humanistic and meliorist, will stimulate, accompany and participate forever in the prodigious saga of human progress.

Chapter 15

EDUCATION AS THE KEY TO TOLERANCE

As it enters the third millennium, the world faces many problems, old and new: political fragmentation of some countries, along ethnic lines, frequently involving mass murders and the creation of hosts of refugees; religious strife (fundamentalism); disease (the AIDS pandemic); hunger (particularly in Africa, but not limited to that continent); the widening chasm that separates the poor countries of the southern hemisphere with the wealthy ones in the north; the rape of the environment deforestation, pollution of seas and the atmosphere; ozone layer depletion; planetary warming; the failure of educational systems everywhere; the persistence of racial bigotry and racially-inspired violence; drug abuse; the list could go on and on.

We might make an attempt to enclose all these issues under three general headings: poverty, fundamentalism, overpopulation. Each is a complex subject, having many aspects and factors at work. They are composite, rather than individual problems.

Poverty is the result of cultural and industrial backwardness, which is itself a concomitant of overpopulation, in the sense that the growth of population is not paralleled by the development of resources.

Overpopulation and poverty provide fertile ground for the growth of religious and nationalist extremism. The search for scapegoats to explain the present hardships suffered by a people results on blind hatred toward racial or cultural minorities. This serves to divert the attention of the public and, instead of looking for the real source of the penury, and finding solutions, the downtrodden individual vents his impotent fury on some suitable scapegoat supplied by the ruling powers.

Overpopulation also results in the depletion of natural resources, some of them irreplaceable. Deforestation, pollution, overexploitation of animal and plant life, are all related to overpopulation and poverty. The inefficient use of resources (e.g., lack of recycling, little of use of replenishing energy sources).

The solution to these grave problems must be found in economic development, but this, in turn, depends on raising the educational level of large segments of the population. Only a body of well-educated people can bring about the development of industry, infrastructure and services at the required level.

Further industrialization without suitable progress in education, particularly technological and scientific, will result in squandering the ever-diminishing reserves of planetary natural resources and will deepen the problems instead of solving them.

Moreover, the fight against bigotry and fanaticism must be fought in the minds of men. Knowledge is the great antidote against prejudice. Education, then, turns out to be the key to the solution of the world's problems in the present circumstances.

Ignorance is the weapon of the totalitarian mentality, which sometimes clothes itself with a religious or nationalist mantle. 'The truth will make you free' is right in more ways than one. That is the reason why dictatorial regimes keep a tight control on education, the media, the press, even the books people can read. The book-burning bonfires of the Hitler era are still etched in our memory. An ignorant populace, easily misled by demagoguery and populism, is the objective of the totalitarian rulers.

The Role of Freemasonry

Traditionally, throughout its long history, symbolic and philosophical Freemasonry has taken a leading role in the promotion of learning and education. From its early beginnings, in the 17th and 18th centuries in England and Scotland, Masons were among the founders of learned academies, such as the Royal Society. Numberless Masons have been active in education at every level from grammar school through university.

Freemasons have been leading educators in Latin America and many other countries. To give just one example, Domingo Faustino Sarmiento, who was a leading Argentinean educational reformer, and later President of his country, was also an active

Mason who became Sovereign Grand Commander of the Supreme Council of the Scottish Rite in Argentine. All his writings and actions and infused with Masonic philosophy.

In Chile, Mexico and elsewhere, Masonry has played a vital role in introducing non-sectarian, universal and free education at the elementary and secondary school levels. In Chile, numerous individual Lodges have organized and manage dozens of private schools that provide high-quality free education to the poor.

An interesting development in the past century has been the appearance of Masonic-supported universities, such as the Free University of Brussels, and the recently-founded La Republica University in Santiago, Chile, created and run by Freemasons. Its name comes from Club de la Republica, as the Grand Lodge of Chile headquarters are known. Other, Masonic-sponsored universities, have been founded or are in the process of being established in various other countries. In the United States, I can mention Girard College, founded by Brother Stephen Girard, and Hamilton College, founded by Samuel Kirkland. I'm sure there are others.

An educated man learns to appreciate the wide range of opinions on any subject. Freemasonry, in addition, allows men of many different professions and backgrounds to meet together in a spirit of cooperation and understanding.

This brings me to the issue of education within the Lodge. All our wonderful principles and ideals are worthless, unless they are actually inculcated in the minds of each Mason. Why are our fundamental principles designated as 'landmarks'? Because they are signposts, they point the way, they are not constraining walls, not anchors, but compass. Freemasonry is not restricted to what goes on within the Lodge room. It has to become a way of life in order for the Initiate to become a true and full-fledged Mason.

The Apprentice's duty is to reflect on his own personality, to detect the faults or failures he may have, and to take the necessary steps to correct them. This, in brief, is what we Masons call 'polishing the rough stone'. The Fellow Craft, having achieved the necessary measure of self-knowledge, widens his cope, extends his sights outside and delves into as many different studies as he is capable of. We designate this as 'studying the seven liberal arts,' but the intention is to encourage the young Mason (young in Masonic age!) to read, discuss, think about matters not connected with his daily routine, his work. Exercising his curiosity, the Fellow Craft discovers aspects of science and art that he ignored. Finally, the Mason reaches the last stage of his three-step Initiation, is raised and becomes a Master Mason.

Master has several meanings. He is, first and foremost, master of himself. Secondly, he's the master and the Fellow Crafts and Apprentices are his pupils. Thirdly, he's the Master Craftsman, building the spiritual Temple of a perfect society.

This describes the threefold orientation of Masonic work: toward himself, toward his Brethren, and toward the world at large. This is symbolized by the three steps approaching the altar.

Hermes, the god of esoteric knowledge, was called Trismegistos, that is, thrice magisterial.

A Mason cannot do Masonic work in isolation. He needs to be within the framework of a Lodge, the Lodge as the assembly of Brethren who compose it. The interaction with his fellow Masons will lead the Mason, if suitably prepared, if he has been duly educated in Masonry, to the practice of tolerance himself, and spreading the message of tolerance everywhere.